New Directions in SHOPPER TECHNOLOGY

New Directions in SHOPPER TECHNOLOGY

SHOPPER TECHNOLOGY INSTITUTE

Edited by John Karolefski, Executive Director

The opinions expressed in this manuscript are solely the opinions of the author and do not represent the opinions or thoughts of the publisher. The author has represented and warranted full ownership and/or legal right to publish all the materials in this book.

New Directions in SHOPPER TECHNOLOGY
All Rights Reserved.
Copyright © 2014 Shopper Technology Institute
v4.0

Cover Photo © 2014 JupiterImages Corporation. All rights reserved - used with permission.

This book may not be reproduced, transmitted, or stored in whole or in part by any means, including graphic, electronic, or mechanical without the express written consent of the publisher except in the case of brief quotations embodied in critical articles and reviews.

Outskirts Press, Inc.
http://www.outskirtspress.com

ISBN: 978-1-4787-0141-5

Outskirts Press and the "OP" logo are trademarks belonging to Outskirts Press, Inc.

PRINTED IN THE UNITED STATES OF AMERICA

Contents

Introduction i

SECTION ONE: SHOPPERS

CHAPTER 1
The Digital Shopper Is Gaining Control 3

CHAPTER 2
From Effort to Entitlement: Evolving Shopper Sentiment ... 15

SECTION TWO: LOYALTY

CHAPTER 3
Making the Leap: Achieving Growth
through Enterprise Loyalty 27

CHAPTER 4
Loyalty Marketing: Where Are We Today? 39

CHAPTER 5
Social Media and CPG Loyalty –
Building Brand Communities 49

SECTION THREE: ENGAGEMENT

CHAPTER 6
The Continuum of Shopper Engagement 61

CHAPTER 7
Winning Shoppers with Big Data on In-Store Behavior ... 71

CHAPTER 8
An Innovation Lens for Retailer Competitive Advantage:
  Grocery Shopping Apps and m-Assisted Retailing 85

CHAPTER 9
Elevating the Voice of the Customer to Increase
  Decision-Making Confidence... 97

SECTION FOUR: ANALYTICS

CHAPTER 10
Marketing Mix Modeling: Regression-Based
  or Agent-Based? 111

CHAPTER 11
Understanding Big Data... 119

CHAPTER 12
The Incredible Dissolving Store Revisited........................... 127

CHAPTER 13
Evolving from Product Warehouses to Retail Experiences ... 137

SECTION FIVE: DIGITAL

CHAPTER 14
The Emergence of Digital Sampling 153

CHAPTER 15
The Multi-Channel Shopper and the Importance
  of Consistency 163

CHAPTER 16
The Emerging Mobile Coupon Ad Unit Standards 171

CHAPTER 17
Five Keys to Securing the Future of Mobile Coupons 175

CHAPTER 18
Coupon Processing Stuck in the '80s 181

CHAPTER 19
Satisfying Customer Need for Accurate and Relevant Product Information for Today and Beyond 189

Index 195

Introduction

It's astonishing how technology has changed the everyday lives of consumers in recent years. The evidence is all around, and many of us have already taken it for granted. Most people own digital devices. Before shopping, many people go online to research products, look for digital coupons, and make a shopping list. They wield smartphones in the store to activate QR codes on displays and packaging. They embrace social media and "like" brands and stores.

Retailers and manufacturers are observing this behavior and analyzing it. The savvy ones are developing programs that engage shoppers with personalized communications. Some recent examples:

- Metro, a Canadian grocery chain, has unveiled what it calls a "digital ecosystem" as a new step in its personalization strategy. The system combines a website and an app for iPhone mobile digital devices. It enables shoppers to manage their purchases before, during and after their trip to the grocery store.

- Members of Safeway's Just for U loyalty program receive personalized offers based on purchase history, along with general coupon offers. The chain is considering eliminating newspaper ads as the technology for Just for U, web and mobile grows.

- Dr Pepper is among the numerous CPG brands successfully connecting with consumers on Facebook and Twitter where promotions are posted. Brands are learning that the true value of their social media efforts is increased sales, and they are optimizing strategies for growth.

- Kellogg is engaging shoppers and boosting its brands with a one-year-old portfolio-wide loyalty program called Family Rewards. Many shoppers have moved from single to multiple categories and brands under Kellogg, based on reward points earned from purchases.

What Is Shopper Technology?

Shopper Technology is broadly defined as tactics and applications that engage and motivate shoppers, analyze their behavior, and enable trading partners to improve their operations. It encompasses everything from social media, loyalty marketing and in-store media to virtual shopping, digital promotions and Big Data analytics.

Merchants and marketers are studying how to serve their mutual customers better. To help the industry in this effort, the providers of Shopper Technology have joined together to share their thought leadership. The result is this book, which picks up where our 2012 book, *The Essentials of Shopper Technology*, left off.

Let's take a look at how the book is organized:

SECTION ONE: Shoppers

Chapter 1, *The Digital Shopper Is Gaining Control*, sets the tone for most of the book by presenting compelling evidence why marketers need to understand the digitally-empowered shopper. Effective segmentation by digital preferences enables marketers to design and execute more productive campaigns.

Chapter 2, *From Effort to Entitlement: Evolving Shopper Sentiment*, examines the shift from effort-based savings to entitlement-based loyalty.

Most shoppers believe that checking out and not receiving a discount for a special to which they are entitled is a customer service defect.

SECTION TWO: Loyalty

Chapter 3, *Making the Leap: Achieving Growth through Enterprise Loyalty,* presents the barrier-breaking concept of Enterprise Loyalty. It requires releasing the power of customer data beyond the marketing department and setting it free across the entire organization.

Chapter 4, *Loyalty Marketing: Where Are We Today?,* provides an update on the many and varied loyalty marketing programs conducted by retailers and manufacturers. These programs range from high tech versions with mobile technology to simple punch cards.

Chapter 5, *Social Media and CPG Loyalty – Building Brand Communities,* explains the benefits of using social media to build brand communities and grow brand loyalty. Several case studies bring this concept to life.

SECTION THREE: Engagement

Chapter 6, *The Continuum of Shopper Engagement,* examines shopper mindsets and how to engage them. There are six different mindsets that make up the continuum. Marketers need to know how to best approach shoppers in each state of mind.

Chapter 7, *Winning Shoppers with Big Data on In-Store Behavior,* focuses on the behavior of shoppers in the store. Both retailers and consumer packaged goods (CPG) manufacturers use an array of data sources to provide insights on different aspects of their business. Data on in-store shopper behavior has become increasingly important.

Chapter 8, *An Innovation Lens for Retailer Competitive Advantage: Grocery Shopping Apps and m-Assisted Retailing,* outlines the evolving connection between the consumer and retailer via digital grocery shopping. Increasingly, it is the consumers' desire to be engaged with the smartphone as they shop.

Chapter 9, *Elevating the Voice of the Customer to Increase Decision-Making Confidence,* discusses how innovative companies are using communities of consent or insight communities as a new gathering approach to elevate the voice of the customer and the marketing and insight team in the organization.

SECTION FOUR: Analytics

Chapter 10, *Marketing Mix Modeling: Regression-Based or Agent-Based?,* examines the strengths and weaknesses of the two forms of the marketing mix model. Knowing these attributes will allow marketing professionals to use the best approach to address their specific issues.

Chapter 11, *Understanding Big Data,* delves into the world of Big Data – both unstructured and structured. Big Data is not just about data volume. It's about the structure and how the industry handles Big Data that is evolving.

Chapter 12, *The Incredible Dissolving Store Revisited,* explains how the boundaries between in-store and out-of-store have become more permeable every day. The walls of the store are becoming more porous with profound implications for brands, retailers and shoppers.

Chapter 13, *Evolving from Product Warehouses to Retail Experiences,* traces the evolution of the grocery store from a self-service product warehouse to a retail shopping experience. Key to the change is the emergence of virtual universes designed to accelerate smart innovation for the CPG and retail industries.

SECTION FIVE: Digital

Chapter 14, *The Emergence of Digital Sampling,* explains why the time is right for digital tactics to ramp up their share of the product sampling business. Consumers are spending more and more time online via PCs, tablets and smartphones, and are receptive to digital offers.

Chapter 15, *The Multi-Channel Shopper and the Importance of Consistency,* outlines the challenge manufacturers and retailers face in making sure that their information is complete, accurate and consistent across a wide variety of channels and digital platforms.

Chapter 16, *The Emerging Mobile Coupon Ad Unit Standards,* provides an update on the initiative by the Mobile Marketing Association to create a Mobile Coupon Ad Units Standard. It is designed to create and launch both retailer-driven store mobile coupons as well as CPG manufacturer-driven coupon campaigns.

Chapter 17, *Five Keys to Securing the Future of Mobile Coupons,* lists the five issues that must be confronted and overcome before widespread adoption of digital coupons by consumers can happen. The goal is seamless electronic clearing of mobile coupons.

Chapter 18, *Coupon Processing Stuck in the '80s,* examines the outdated, inefficient and costly retail practice of handling coupons that begs to be addressed. Real-time electronic coupon validation is the change that is needed today.

Chapter 19, *Satisfying Customer Need for Accurate and Relevant Product Information for Today and Beyond,* presents the case for protecting the integrity of brands across all digital platforms. Brand owners are not in the position to dedicate production resources to photography and data aggregation efforts.

Closing Thoughts

These insightful chapters were provided by the sponsoring members of the Shopper Technology Institute. I salute them for sharing their expertise with the industry. Also, a shout-out goes to Linda Winick, STI's Director of Operations, whose dedication and unrelenting effort were responsible for the production of this book.

Shopper Technology is driving change throughout the retail and consumer goods industry. Those executives who incorporate the new tactics and solutions into their organization will advance in today's competitive environment. Sadly, the others will be left behind.

As Shopper Technology moves in new directions, consider this book as your guide to change and the chapters as signposts along the way. The destination is what you make of it.

John Karolefski
Executive Director
Shopper Technology Institute
www.ShopperTech.org

SECTION ONE
SHOPPERS

CHAPTER 1

The Digital Shopper Is Gaining Control

By Bob Tomei

The shopper is in control today. Products do not drive top-line sales and bottom-line profit growth; shoppers do! To best grasp this transformation in shopper marketing, it is critical to understand the evolution in the manufacturer-retailer-shopper relationship.

Prior to the 1960s, consumer packaged goods (CPG) manufacturers dominated the relationship with retailers and consumers. Brand managers decided which products their companies would manufacture; national television, radio and print advertising campaigns would inform consumers that to be upwardly mobile, every household must have this brand of soup or that brand of paper towel.

Then a shift occurred. Computers and database programs allowed the retailers that actually "touched" the shopper on a daily basis to learn what categories, products, trips, store layouts and promotions shoppers preferred. Other retail innovators realized that by understanding the detailed needs of shoppers, they could market and differentiate themselves versus simply serving as another distribution point for manufacturers.

Even as retailers were wresting control over the manufacturer-retailer-shopper relationship, a new set of trends was emerging that would result in yet another change to this relationship. Shoppers were now in charge. Shoppers that had marched in lock step to buy aspirational brands and conform with the "norms" of their friends and/or neighborhood began to worry less about "fitting in" and worry more about their individual circumstances. Some were worried about simply putting food on the table; others wanted to buy more sustainable products; and others wanted to eat healthy.

Today, social media has added a new dimension to shopper empowerment—the ability to offer and share information in real time. Shoppers increasingly rely on third-party information providers through collaborative product reviews, rankings, ratings and price-comparisons to research the brands and channels that best meet their needs.

The ability to understand and directly communicate with individual shoppers is an exciting opportunity. From reading and writing product reviews to searching for coupons, shoppers are increasingly turning to the internet to plan and execute shopping trips. But CPG marketers are still struggling to assess online behavior and employ meaningful digital strategies. Should we engage with shoppers online? Which consumers should be targeted? And how?

The new path-to-purchase provides many more touch points to connect with your most valuable consumers and shoppers

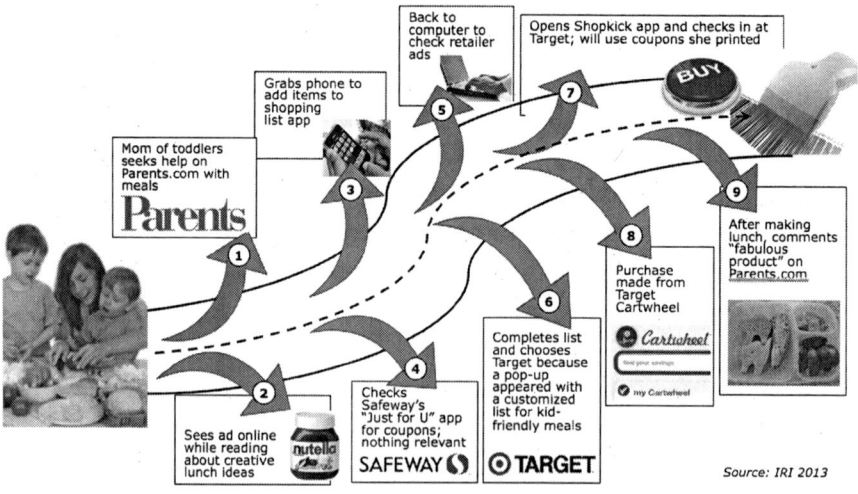

Source: IRI 2013

Effective segmentation by digital preferences enables marketers to design and execute more productive campaigns by understanding both the attitudes of shoppers as well as the devices and media on which they prefer to receive information. More specifically, marketers should:

- Use digital segmentation to analyze various shoppers' attitudes toward digital devices and online media, and to explore the role that technology plays in their shopping behaviors.

- Single out the groups that present the greatest digital marketing opportunities and provide an in-depth assessment of their preferences and how they can be targeted.

- Engage marketing and advertising agencies in a research-driven conversation to develop meaningful digital strategies.

Digital Segmentation

In April 2013, for the second year in a row, IRI surveyed its 100,000 household Consumer Network panel, examining attitudes about digital media. The study revealed five distinct segments of active Internet users, each exhibiting unique online behaviors. The segments are broken down as follows:

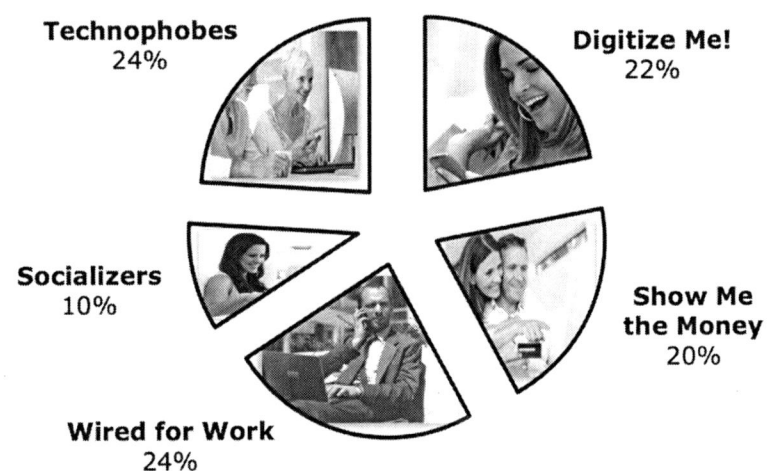

Active Internet Users Exhibit Diverse Digital Behavior

- Technophobes 24%
- Digitize Me! 22%
- Show Me the Money 20%
- Wired for Work 24%
- Socializers 10%

Source: IRI DigitaLink™ Segmentation Survey 2012

Technophobes: Technophobes are the least online-savvy group. This older segment of the population accounts for 24 percent of those surveyed, has a median income of $43,000, and uses the internet primarily for email. They prefer face-to-face communication over online interaction and tend to feel overwhelmed by technology. Compared with the general U.S. population, Technophobes are more likely to buy health, beauty and cosmetic (HBC) products aimed at older demographics such as vitamins, dentures, adult incontinence and gastrointestinal products. They also purchase more wine, baking nuts, pantyhose/nylons and outdoor/lawn/fertilizer products than the general population.

Socializers: Accounting for 10 percent of shoppers, Socializers use the internet primarily as a means of communication, specifically social media and online dating. Socializers do not see the internet as a primary shopping resource. They seldom search for coupons or research new products online, and do not compare prices online before purchasing in store.

Compared with the total survey sample, Socializers are more likely to buy products related to smoking and coffee drinking including cigarettes, lighters, coffee creamers and refrigerated coffee/teas. They are also over-index for denture and adult incontinence products and have the lowest median income—$27,000—of all the groups.

Wired for Work: Twenty-four percent of those surveyed fall under the Wired for Work segment and use digital media primarily for work. These shoppers are highly proficient with new digital devices. Nearly 3 in 4 own a smartphone, but they are not interested in using technology for shopping. Wired for Work shoppers rarely read about new products online, comment on blogs or "like" products on Facebook.

Though this is a technologically advanced group, they are not likely to be attracted to new marketing methods. This is unfortunate as they are the wealthiest group, with a median income of $76,000. The average Wired for Work household spends $3,484 on CPG products per year, $172 more than the average household in the survey. This group buys more personal appearance-related products than average consumers, including suntan products, cosmetic accessories, blades, hair styling gel and mousse. They also over-index for diapers, baby accessories, refrigerated lunches and pastas.

Show Me the Money: Show Me the Money shoppers make up 20 percent of the market. With a median income of $50,000, this group uses digital media specifically to save money. They frequently download coupons and often compare prices and product details before making a purchase. Show Me the Money shoppers are also comfortable buying and selling products online.

Although they embrace the internet, these shoppers have not gravitated to smartphones or other mobile devices. This group is not very involved with social media, so they are not likely to share product news with friends. These shoppers are slightly older than the other groups, but are wealthier, more educated, and more likely to embrace digital technologies than Technophobes. This sector is more likely than average to purchase various goods, including cigarettes, hair color products, cat food and litter, salad dressing, and adult incontinence products.

Digitize Me!: With a 10 percent increase in size in just over a year, this group now accounts for 22 percent of shoppers. This is the digital shopper group that CPG and retail decision makers should focus on. Digitize Me! shoppers are fully engaged in the online experience; they often shop online and rely heavily on the internet as a means of discovering new products.

Digitize Me! shoppers are the most likely to interact with companies and brands on social networks. They share opinions, photos and videos through social media and often write blogs and product reviews. In fact, online activities on media sites such as Linkedin, Facebook, Twitter and photo sharing sites have almost doubled since the 2011 survey.

The Digitize Me! group frequently searches for online coupons and is most likely to sell products online through sites like eBay and Etsy. As the youngest group, Digitize Me! shoppers are extremely comfortable with technology. They are constantly "plugged in," bringing the latest digital devices, especially smartphones, wherever they go. Digitize Me! shoppers are highly educated and have the second-highest median income—$65,000—after Wired for Work. This segment is highly over-represented in the baby and beauty categories. They buy more diapers, baby food, baby accessories, baby needs products, moist towelettes, razors, cosmetic accessories, hair styling gel and mousse than the average shopper surveyed.

Digitized Shoppers Hold the Best Opportunity

Of the five shopper segments, only two provide significant short-term opportunities for online marketing success: Show Me the Money and Digitize Me!, which represent 20 percent and 22 percent of shoppers respectively. These two categories are most likely to research CPG categories online and spend a greater percentage of their money online overall. The other three segments – Technophobes, Socializers and Wired for Work -- make up 58 percent of the online population, but unfortunately do not offer much near-term online marketing potential. Given their online behaviors, these groups would not be receptive to online marketing tactics, and should not be a primary online target.

Online Shopping Behaviors

When preparing to make a purchase, the five shopper segments each exhibit unique online behaviors. Digitize Me! and Wired for Work shoppers are most likely to start their shopping process online, often via mobile phone. Like the Show Me the Money group, these two segments conduct online research and also browse the in-store selection, mixing traditional shopping behaviors and more technologically advanced strategies. Digitize Me! and Show Me the Money shoppers are most likely to research CPG products online, including beauty products, over-the-counter medications, non-perishable, fresh and frozen foods, household cleaning products and household paper goods. The Digitize Me! group is most in-depth with online preparation, often searching for video product demos or online rebates before arriving at a final decision.

Digitize Me! and Show Me the Money shoppers are most likely to make actual online purchases. They are comfortable buying online from numerous retail outlets including mass merchandisers, department stores, drug stores, club stores, grocery stores and dollar stores. After an online purchase, these groups are also likely to rate the items they bought or write online reviews.

Online Activity: Pre-Shopping Behaviors

	DIGITIZE ME!	SHOW ME THE MONEY	WIRED FOR WORK	SOCIALIZERS	TECHNOPHOBES
Begin the Product Research Process Online	⬆	⬆	■	⬇	⬇
Browse In-Store/ Buy Online	⬆	⬆	⬇	⬇	⬇
Look for Grocery Product Coupons Online	⬆	⬆	⬇	⬇	⬇
Compare Prices Online Before Buying	⬆	⬆	■	⬇	⬇
Learn About Product Online Then Go to Store To Purchase	⬆	⬆	■	⬇	⬇

⬇ = Index Low   ⬆ = Index High   ■ = No Skew

Source: IRI DigitaLink™ Segmentation Survey 2012

Digitize Me!, Show Me the Money and, to a lesser degree, Wired for Work are the three shopper segments most likely to respond positively to online marketing campaigns.

Shopper Marketing Activation

Using their knowledge of the five shopper segments, marketers can turn these insights into action through aggressive shopper marketing activation. This process allows CPG marketers to single out an individual segment, deliver targeted campaigns that resonate with that segment and increase ROI.

The three core steps are as follows:

- *Identify:* Examine the brand's consumer base to determine which of the segments is the top priority. Consider key consumer groups and high-value shoppers. Determine where they live, where they shop, and what media and digital technologies they use.

- *Activate Media Messaging and Consumption*: Create media campaigns, direct-to-consumer programs, focused messaging and concentrated content, and deliver these online through the most effective channels.

- *Activate Retail Channels, Banners and Stores:* Use the information uncovered about target markets, geographies and favored retailers to reach shoppers through the right retail channels, banners and stores.

In addition, marketers must also be able to answer basic questions, such as who is the target shopper, how does a product's consumer profile compare to a competitor's product, what are the leisure, lifestyle and media habits of the target consumer at the national or local market level, and what categories and products have the greatest opportunity with core consumers and buyers. Products such as IRI ShopperSights™ can provide a new level of granularity, including household-level scoring, predictive attribute modeling, POS-driven opportunity assessments and multi-attribute, weighted retail trade areas.

The following case study illustrates the shopper marketing activation process and demonstrates its importance:

A new, eco-friendly, high-end dishwashing detergent entered the market. With no existing online marketing strategy, brand managers sought to promote the new detergent digitally, but were unsure of their targets and how to begin. To engage consumers online effectively, brand managers needed to evaluate their shopper base to identify priority segments. The decision makers could activate that knowledge through the proper media messaging and retail channels.

Using digital segmentation, the detergent brand determined that 66 percent of its volume sales came from Digitize Me! and Show Me the Money shoppers. Since these two segments were the largest purchasers by volume sales and the most engaged online, they were ideal targets for the company's initial digital outreach.

To gain precise details, brand managers focused first on Show Me the Money, determining that these shoppers were most concentrated in West Virginia, Utah, Nevada and Texas. Realizing the importance of localized digital campaigns, decision makers looked at West Virginia specifically, finding that Show Me the Money shoppers there preferred Foodland and Kroger grocery stores. Examining the media habits of the Show Me the Money group, they found that news and sports websites were popular, and online coupons were effective activators. Repeating the "identify" steps for the Digitize Me! segment, brand managers found that Whole Foods and Fresh & Easy were the most popular grocers, while the most-visited websites were all social: MySpace, Gmail, Facebook and YouTube.

Since brand managers effectively identified key shopper groups, where they live, what stores they frequent, and what media they enjoy, they knew exactly who to target, and how. The brand realized the significant attitudinal and behavioral differences between the Show Me the Money and Digitize Me! groups, and created tailored campaigns targeted to the media each views with distinct offers designed to motivate the shopper to action.

The identification of the geographic areas where these two segments were the most concentrated allowed marketers to set priorities via a geo-targeting mechanism, particularly for digital media campaigns. A sophisticated targeting platform enabled marketers to expose only those who live in targeted areas, and did so anonymously via the shopper's computer IP address. In addition, digital marketers were able to find similar shoppers to the Digitize Me! and Show Me the Money segments through their cookie pool, searching for common denominators such as age and income.

Based on store preference findings, decision makers attracted Digitize Me! shoppers with coupons for a leading specialty grocery chain. They also launched a social media campaign on Facebook, offering coupons to shoppers who encouraged their friends to "like" the brand's page. This effort drove sales in target regions and increased Facebook "likes."

For Show Me the Money, the detergent brand purchased local advertisements on specific news and sports websites that were popular with that segment. The ads included a link to download coupons for the new dishwashing detergent. Using analytics tools, the brand determined that the ad received a high volume of clicks and also saw product sales increase in their target regions.

The detergent brand succeeded in identifying and understanding its key shopper groups and converting that knowledge to activation. Brand managers earned significantly higher ROI for their digital campaigns than if they had treated all digital shoppers the same.

As illustrated, each digital segment holds different opinions and is affected by different motivators, which will require different treatment. The first and most important step is to classify your customer base to determine whether digital marketing is right for a product or channel. If the majority of your customers are Technophobes or Socializers, attempting growth through a digital strategy is not likely to bear the ROI managers will expect.

However, if research reveals a product or channel's shoppers exhibit the characteristics of Digitize Me! or Show Me the Money (and in some cases Wired for Work shoppers), now is the time to start engaging these shoppers online. If possible, start with outreach to the

Digitize Me! Group, as they will be the most receptive and are also the most likely to pass on messaging to others. Above all, targeting is key. It is essential to learn where target shoppers are geographically, where they shop and what websites they frequent, and then use that information to craft a precisely tailored digital marketing plan.

Bob Tomei is President of IRI Consumer and Shopper Insights. For more information: www.iriworldwide.com

Source:
IRI 2011 and 2012 DigitaLink™ Segmentation Survey

CHAPTER 2

From Effort to Entitlement: Evolving Shopper Sentiment

By John Ross

Think back to the last time you stood in line in a supermarket, a restaurant check-out stand, or even in line to buy tickets. Now imagine that the shopper in front of you throws down a slip of paper – maybe several – entitling them to pay a lower price than you. "Wait a minute," you think. "I shop this store all the time. I have their loyalty card in my wallet. But because they have a piece a paper and I do not, they pay less? How is that fair?"

For the longest time, shoppers understood this retail phenomenon: That shopper in front of you, they research deals, they go online, they sift through the newspaper for coupons. Heck, they even watch Extreme Couponing on cable. And you might say, "If I wanted to work that hard, I could have saved money, too."

But if you are like many shoppers today, that scenario no longer meets their expectations. You might think, "I've been shopping that store for years. My money spends just like anyone else's. Why should I have to put in so much effort to get savings on stuff I buy all the time? I shouldn't have to work to save money."

If you feel this way, you are not alone. Increasingly, shoppers are changing their expectations. They are driven by experiences in other industries and by experiences with online technology that not only remembers them, but serves them with customized experiences based on their shopping behavior. They are increasingly becoming frustrated with a world where the effort to save has been pushed onto the shoulders of the shopper.

"If I am a loyal customer," many say, "why do I have to hunt and peck to find the values? And, if I buy items that qualify for a discount, why don't you (the retailer) automatically match my purchase to discounts?"

This shift from effort-based savings to entitlement-based loyalty is not new, but it is stronger and more engrained than ever. In fact, most shoppers now say that checking out and not receiving a discount for a special to which they are entitled is a customer service defect.

Industry research companies like Inmar Analytics can see this seachange in consumer sentiment. It is a shift from effort to entitlement. The question is, how can brands and retailers harness this new sentiment, bend it to their will and grow their market share?

The Amazonification of Retail

Ever read about the Amazon tribe from the ancient world? You remember, the war women who raided cities, enslaved males, and flipped the entire ideal of the classically understood roles of men and women? The ancient Greeks and Romans were terrified of the Amazons. They represented a complete upheaval in their power base. The Amazonian ideal positioned women as powerful rather than weak; as in-control rather than subservient; as skilled rather than uneducated… a profile that retailers and shopper marketing types will instantly recognize: The engaged and empowered shopper.

Today we have access to more product information, previous purchaser reviews, warranty and repair records – all at the click of mouse (or swipe of a smartphone screen). Shoppers today know everything from insider information on nutrition to deal cost. They often are more knowledgeable about the products and services retailers sell than the sales associates themselves. Internet and mobile technology means that shoppers can dictate the terms of engagement with retailers and brands, choosing where, where and how they want to access their wares.

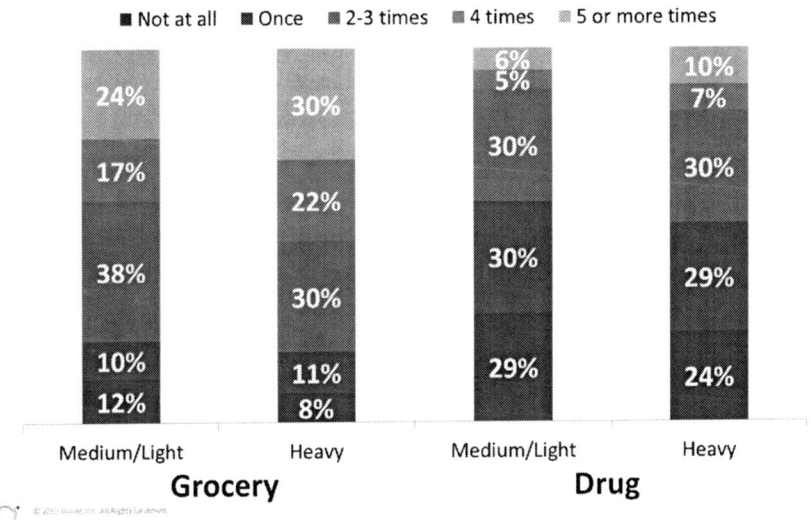

Shoppers have doubled the number of sources they use to make a purchase decision in the last few years (*Shopper Sciences*, 2011 Macro Shopper Study), driven in part by easier access to information. But the fact that they can get all this data does not mean that it actually influences the decisions they make.

How do we reach this shopper? What does he or she want? Inmar Analytics reveals emerging shopper behavior in the 2013 Shopper Behavior Study, released in the first quarter 2013. Based on surveys of more than 3,000 shoppers, the study reveals how shoppers engage with technology while pre-shopping and in-store, the types of coupons they use, how they discover and acquire coupons, their attitudes toward coupon use and overall retail satisfaction. Several findings have been surprisingly consistent across categories. Here is what shoppers had to say:

18 | NEW DIRECTIONS IN SHOPPER TECHNOLOGY

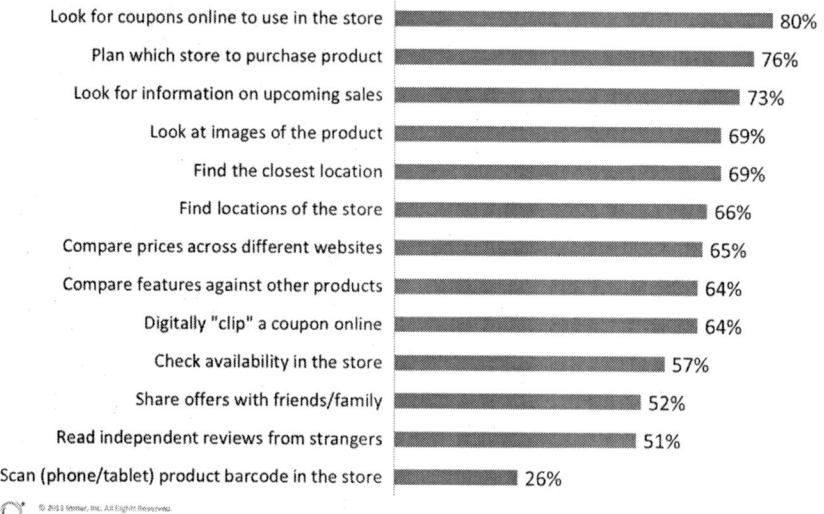

- **I Have to Be Smarter:** Whether due to economic pressure, time constraints or simply a hunger for information, shoppers are turning to readily accessible content through myriad digital devices. Eighty percent looked for coupons to use in-store prior to their trip, and said the process made them feel smarter. More than a quarter relied on their mobile device for decision support while in-store. Retailers and manufacturers that embrace digital and mobile technology have the opportunity to engage with shoppers well in advance and through the entire decision / purchase cycle – not just through their own properties and efforts, but by understanding competitive and complementary solutions in their space. "Know your frenemy" is a common expression. Your customer is smarter; your brand needs to be smarter, too.

- **I Want It to Be Easier:** This is where the most pronounced change in shopper sentiment seems to be occurring: From effort to entitlement. Previously, shoppers understood the deal-seeking game. They were willing to put in a little time and effort, and be rewarded with discounts. Now, fully 65 percent of the shoppers we surveyed do not believe they should be required to work to find deals – at all. This is the essence of Amazonification: Shoppers expect retailers to know their purchase history, purchase frequency and reward them accordingly in exchange for getting their business.

- *My Loyalty Must Be Re-Earned*: It's not that loyalty has eroded; it is reevaluated each time by the site experience and by the store experience. Was the site easily navigable? Was the physical store clean? Was the product as advertised? Did I get the deals I deserve, or did I get ripped off? The proliferation of crowd-sourced product reviews has made even the most passive shoppers incredibly savvy. Reliably habitual behaviors can be disrupted by just the slightest inkling of curiosity. But now that information is so widespread, shoppers *still* do not want to have to work to find it. In fact, 78 percent believe all available coupons should be automatically applied to their purchase with no effort. They want it to be easy, and they reward the brands and retailers that effectively deliver that experience, each time. That is loyalty in the 21st century.

Evolving Couponer Profiles

Conventional wisdom surrounding the "typical couponer" profile has always been suspect. It's not that "mid-thirties, female, 2.5 kids, buying for the household" is inaccurate; it's simply not very helpful – too broad and general to provide actionable value. Inmar's research findings and data suggest a more nuanced and fragmented space, with coupon use occurring across demographic and economic spectra. The (over)simplified, (stereo) typical couponer profile is beginning to be displaced by smaller, more notable profile characteristics observed across studies.

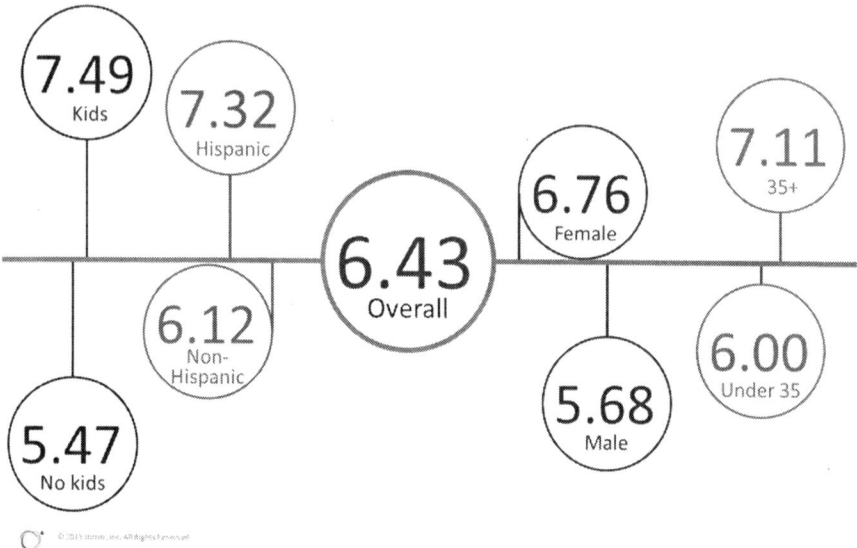

Inmar Analytics has identified four shopper types whose coupon use patterns may be insightful for fellow promotion professionals. They are:

The Heavy Couponer: Similar to the "typical couponer" profile, the Heavy Couponer is difficult to (accurately) describe using conventional ethno- and demographic terms. Defined as a shopper who uses coupons on more than half their shopping trips, Heavies transcend categorization other than their common coupon use. However, as 59 percent of shoppers surveyed met this criteria (having used coupons for more than half of their shopping trips), they are a force to be reckoned with and worthy of scrutiny.

The Heavy Couponer is (naturally) coupon savvy. Not only do they tend to utilize more coupon methods and sources (7.85) than average (4.37) during pre-shop planning, the Heavy Couponer understands how to "game" the system to maximize available discounts (which groceries double coupons, and up to what value; what drug retailers permit the stacking of store offers with manufacturer coupons, etc.) which plays a significant role in retailer selection. The Heavy Couponer is well-versed in coupon mechanics, not fazed by complex, cross-ruff promotions, and is generally willing to participate in loyalty programs. However, they expect personalized, contextually relevant offers in exchange for the shopping data they allow the retailer to observe.

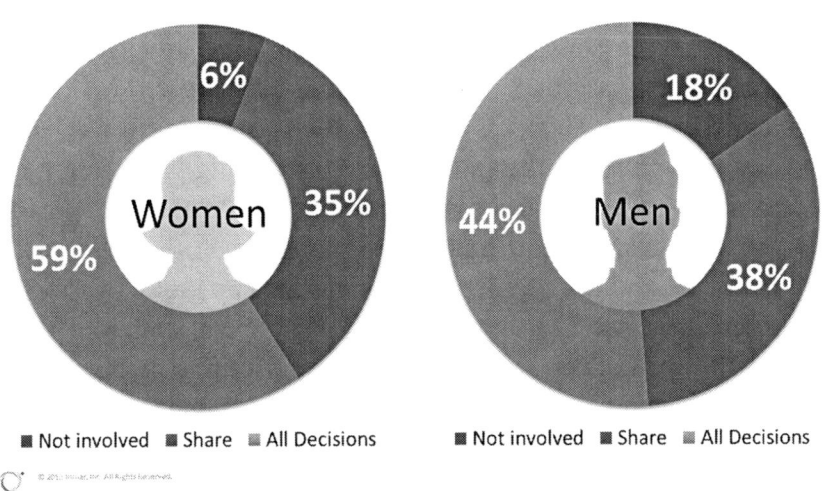

The Mansumer: The Mansumer serves as a basic counterpoint to the conventional wisdom of the "typical couponer" profile. While men's shopping behavior varies widely by category, they are seemingly more willing to self-identify as coupon users than in recent years. Men are also increasingly serving as the primary grocery shopper in their household, particularly when children are present; 51 percent of fathers surveyed by Yahoo!/DB5 indicated that they were responsible for grocery shopping for their household. Some remnants of the anecdotal "typical male shopper" profile (get in/get out, mission focused, not wandering the aisles) persist; however, men, in general, use fewer coupon methods overall and are less inclined to hunt/seek coupon offers than the average shopper. Essentially, they are less willing to put in the work to find offers; they want coupons loaded automatically to their loyalty card without having to think about it or plan for it. Rather than seeing this as a relic of days gone by, this is actually a sign of shopping behavior to come – and not just for the Mansumer. Shoppers increasingly expect retailers to meet the standards set by companies like Amazon: Make it easy, know me, know what I want, give me offers for the items I want. This is the sea change in consumer sentiment occurring today from effort to entitlement. Who knew the Mansumer would be an early adopter?

Hispanic Shoppers: Among the ethno- and demographic groups surveyed by Inmar's Shopper Behavior Studies, a few key insights were uncovered for this group of native Spanish speakers. For instance, although Hispanic Shoppers self-identified as having lower education and income levels than study averages, the digital adoption rates scored significantly higher than study norms – particularly mobile. The mobile device is an increasingly crucial form of engagement for any marketer, and is certainly appropriate for this group of shoppers. Marketers who seek to target Hispanic Shoppers, and who do not have unlimited budgets, would be wise to prioritize mobile engagement into their digital media strategy: Text/short-code programs (for feature phones and smartphones) as well as apps and mobile site optimization (for smartphones). This is particularly relevant for retailers in the dollar, drug and convenience classes of trade, where Hispanic shoppers surveyed expressed a preference for visiting. Interestingly, while Hispanic Shoppers spent more in mass and drug channels than study averages, they reported the least amount of loyalty to any particular chain. Like the Mansumer's desire for simplicity, this is also consistent with the overall "Amazonification" of retail: Shopping as a commoditized behavior, perpetually loaned out to retailers that have earned the privilege of today's visit – but are not guaranteed ongoing loyalty.

Digital Natives: There is a temptation to group these shoppers into the generational "Millennial" bucket, but that would be a mistake. While the groups certainly share several overlapping characteristics – Digital

Natives skewed younger than survey averages, more likely to have a college degree, higher incomes, etc. – they are not synonymous. Digital Natives are simply shoppers for whom technology and devices have become pervasive and interwoven aspects of their everyday lives. For retail, this means pre-shop planning and in-store engagement: Digital Natives are naturally researching brands and products ahead of time, as well as performing price comparisons at shelf. A decade ago, this group would have been the "early adopters" of mobile technology. Their stated desires today may be decent predictors of functionality that will be commonplace ten years from now: in-aisle navigation, mobile checkout (bypass the register) and, yes, entirely paperless digital coupons that are discovered, acquired, presented, redeemed (and settled) all via one single mobile device. Smartphone users surveyed even relied on more coupon methods (7.12) than non-smartphone users (5.12), but heavily preferred online/digital methods.

John Ross is president of Inmar Analytics. Inmar is a technology company that operates intelligent commerce networks. Our Promotion, Supply Chain and Healthcare platforms enable commerce, generate meaningful data and offer growth-minded leaders actionable analytics and execution with real-time visibility. For more information: www.inmar.com

SECTION TWO
LOYALTY

CHAPTER 3

Making the Leap: Achieving Growth through Enterprise Loyalty

By Bryan Pearson

Back in the mid 1990s, the Canadian marketplace was facing a gas crisis that had little to do with prices, fuel shortages or taxes. Instead, this crisis involved locations, and it took a loyalty program to help fix it.

The market was overstored, meaning far too many stations were operating along our roadways, and a disproportionate number of them did not meet consumer expectations for greater convenience, pay-at-the-pump, and ease of use. The industry was overdue for rationalization. So its many smaller, outdated locations were closed, relocated or retrofitted into larger, more profitable self-service stations.

Enter the fuel chain Shell, which set a rather ambitious goal: It planned to reduce its network by 20%, from 2,500 to roughly 2,000 sites, while also renovating a significant number of its remaining stations to stay competitive. Shell planned to do this through its partnership with the AIR MILES Reward Program, operated by my company, the Canadian loyalty marketer LoyaltyOne. AIR MILES, with almost 10 million members, is one of the world's largest coalition loyalty programs – a collaboration of scores of merchant partners through which consumers can earn and redeem reward points.

Still, even with the partnership, Shell's plan was ambitious. For any retail organization, maintaining market and customer share while reducing locations is about as difficult as changing the wings on an airplane in mid-flight. But Shell was already well down the customer management path and, through its partnership with AIR MILES, had a secret weapon: Access to customer information that represented more than 60% of its sales volume. Shell's challenge was to mine this data to accomplish three critical tasks:

- Identify which Shell sites should be closed for renovation

- Transfer customers of those closed stations to nearby Shell locations, essentially retaining business and market share

- Ensure that the renovated gas stations, once reopened, quickly recaptured those relocated customers.

To achieve this task, we helped Shell dig into the numbers to identify established shopping practices, define driving patterns, and design a marketing and awareness program to direct its consumers to new locations. We found, for instance, that members of the AIR MILES program accounted for about 60% of each location's total revenue, and of those customers, half generated 86% of those sales. This was the target market. By understanding their behaviors, including the customers' shopping patterns not only at Shell but also at the other merchants within our loyalty coalition, we could predict which Shell sites these customers would turn to once their regular locations closed.

The approach was elegant in its simplicity and focus. First, we alerted customers through direct mail and in-store marketing of a location's upcoming renovations and guided them to the nearest (and most likely) alternate site. Then, to give customers an incentive to stick with Shell during the shift, we offered double AIR MILES for purchases made at that second station. Post renovation, Shell provided a suite of welcome-back offers, including direct mailers offering double and triple reward miles, as well as a site re-opening announcement to encourage customers back to their newly renovated and preferred location.

There were pre-existing challenges. A gas station renovation typically takes six weeks. If a customer fills up once a week, that translates to six occasions when he or she could choose a different brand. It was critical to identify the right alternate station and motivate Shell's customers to change behavior and make it their new destination as quickly as possible.

So what happened? As a result of good planning and effective data use, Shell was able to retain about 75% of its customer volume during renovations, up from the industry standard of 25%. Shell's renovated stores were able to regain their former volume in half the projected time, and in response to offers, customers actually increased their overall spending by an average of 7%. Yes, you read that correctly. Shell closed a customer's most frequently used location, and that customer actually spent *more* at Shell during the renovation by driving *further* to buy its gas.

How did Shell over-deliver on experience? It communicated openly with loyal customers, recognizing their brand affiliation and talking to them as Shell "insiders." It sent communications that openly acknowledged the inconvenience caused by the construction. And, to help offset that disruption, it offered double or triple miles as an incentive to stick it out with Shell during the renovation.

Throughout the process, Shell evolved from Canada's least efficient major fuel retailer (ranking fourth) to the most efficient, on the basis of volume per site, a position it still holds today. All this while maintaining market share in what could have been a major period of customer churn and dissatisfaction among its most loyal customers.

What Loyalty? Is My Customer Cheating On Me?

Thanks to success stories like that at Shell, the potential value generated by customer loyalty is a subject that has received a great deal of attention in recent years. In the United States, the number of programs from 2010 to 2012 alone has advanced almost 27%, to 2.65 billion from 2 billion.[1] Yet most organizations have little or no idea how loyal their customers are.

Those companies that do try to measure "loyalty" typically end up measuring customer satisfaction instead, and that can be risky. Think of customer satisfaction as the Trojan horse of loyalty: If you accept customer satisfaction as true loyalty, which is a generous gift, then you trick yourself into believing all is well and right between you and your customers. The scary truth, however, is that many of your "satisfied" customers are simply tolerating your services until they can find a competitor that offers a better price, service or location. For every loyal customer who promotes your brand, there is another whose bags are packed, waiting for the next slightly better feature or benefit to come along. Loyalty is hard earned and nurtured every day. It doesn't just come stumbling through the gate.

In fact, it's worth distinguishing upfront between two kinds of loyalty: behavioral and emotional. What we deem to be "satisfied" customers often fall under the former.

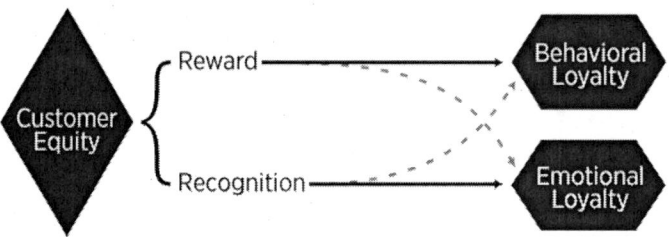

Behavioral loyalty simply reflects purchasing behavior and is typically motivated by rewards. When customers maintain their shopping frequency and purchasing patterns, they are deemed "loyal" to the company because they shop with something close to the average consumer's spending behaviors. If asked in a survey, that customer is likely to tell you what you want to hear. Products are fine. Service is fine. Prices are fine. He or she

---

[1] 2013 COLLOQUY Loyalty Census, June 2013

has no bone to pick with you, but as soon as a better option is presented, that same shopper will drop you like a bag of hammers.

Behavioral loyalty is a very strong indication of convenience, price advantage or even a lack of viable competition, but it falls short as a measure of customer engagement. Behavioral loyalty is fragile and fleeting.

Emotional loyalty, on the other hand, exists within a sustained customer relationship and is based on the company's capacity to directly recognize the customer's contributions. That customer is yours, despite very attractive offers from the competition. Although it is arguably the most solid measure of future customer value, the marriage of emotion and commercial results is hard for most financial analysts to conceive.

Research by the Gallup organization has been helpful, providing clear evidence that a customer who is emotionally loyal to a business is more valuable than one who is only behaviorally loyal, or satisfied. In a surprising study of customers of an international credit card provider, researchers John Fleming and Jim Asplund found that "rationally satisfied" customers performed only slightly better than those who described themselves as "dissatisfied," demonstrating nearly identical spending behavior.[2]

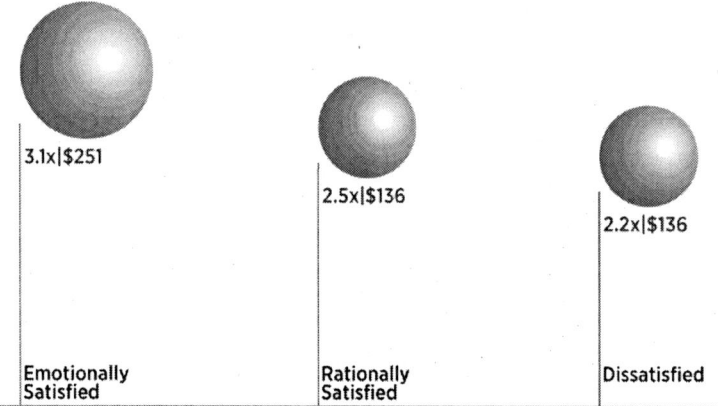

Bubble elevation indicates average per-month credit card use; bubble size indicates average monthly spend in dollars.

Source: Human Sigma: Managing the Employee-Customer Encounter, Gallup Press, 2007

---

[2] *Human Sigma: Managing the Employee-Customer Encounter*, Gallup Press, 2007.

"Emotionally satisfied" customers, meanwhile, increased their spending by 67% over a 12-month period, compared with a mere 8% among the rationally satisfied customers. The data also showed that emotionally satisfied customers used their credit cards 3.1 times per month and spent $251 on average, while rationally satisfied customers used their cards 2.5 times a month for an average spending of $136. What's more, Gallup found that this "emotional advocacy" was alive and well across multiple consumer categories, including retail banking, hospitality, airlines and retail.

Customer Intimacy, Your Emotional Rescue
Quantifying the value of emotional loyalty is an important first step to get organizational alignment, but then comes the nuts and bolts of obtaining it and the organization-wide follow through. To achieve emotional loyalty and, ultimately, customer intimacy, a company needs to apply some rigor to the data collection and analysis and understand the demands, inspirations and aspirations of its customers. With the benefit of advanced analytical techniques, we can design more relevant and meaningful communications, products, services, rewards and experiences. These are the anchors of customer loyalty and when done right, they drive financial performance.

It's harder than it looks, but not as hard as you think. Customer behaviors are predictable, customer experiences are measureable, and a dashboard of tools is available to any marketer with a reasonably robust database. At the end of the day, the biggest hurdle will be strategic focus. Pursuing a customer-intimate strategy requires a fundamental shift of focus from product to customer. This means getting all the functional groups involved. When you start by mapping the customer journey, you soon realize you need every part of the organization that touches the customer to be on board.

Although we may have a more exact measure of emotional loyalty some day, the power of today's data is highly predictive. I can safely say we're past the point of reading tea leaves to plan customer strategy. Case in point: One of LoyaltyOne's grocery clients recently asked us why it was not selling more meat at one of its urban stores. By examining the data from the loyalty card program, we identified that its key customer segments for that location were college students, young singles and low-income couples. When we recommended adding single-serve, convenient and lower-priced cuts of meat, sales in the beef category rose 12%.

This strategy not only helped to prevent an under-served group of customers from seeking shopping alternatives, but it strengthened their relationship with the retailer. Such small, tactical initiatives can have a cumulative effect on customer intimacy over time.

But despite huge data stores, many companies are still conditioned to use their customer information to accelerate this week's product sales, not to map shopper needs. It's a hard habit to break. There are a few well-noted exceptions: Best Buy, Amazon and Tesco have all built analytical engines around their customers. But a good number of companies are still doing fairly rudimentary things with their data. And despite the best intentions of marketers to focus on the consumer, most companies find it difficult to justify the associated costs, especially when the resulting emotional loyalty is hard to measure.

So what are they to do?

Enterprise Loyalty: One Small Step for Marketing, One Giant Leap for Loyalty

Such a commitment requires more than tactical top-down strategizing; it takes an organization-wide transformation that redirects its focus from the product to the customer. It is what we call "Enterprise Loyalty," and it is a barrier-breaking concept. It requires releasing the power of customer data beyond the marketing department, where it is kept under wraps, and setting it free across the entire organization, from purchasing to finance and from the corporate office to the store clerk. The goal of Enterprise Loyalty is not simply enhancing the customer experience, but transforming it.

When customer data becomes a shared currency across the enterprise, it can inform decisions throughout the company, including merchandising and product design to store location, layout and pricing. Companies that use this approach are surpassing traditional loyalty marketing programs or one-off campaigns. They are taking a more holistic approach to the way the entire organization responds to their customers.

But make no mistake; such change can be demanding. Each business unit is committed to conventional data sets, and your colleagues may not lay out the welcome mat when you look to fold customer data into the formula. Members of the research group love their random samples; why would they want to re-calibrate testing with customer value segments? Retail merchants live and die by year-over-year measures such as same-store sales, average selling price, inventory turns and items per basket.

We will need to demonstrate the power of the data when unit measures are combined with customer measures. To do this, we have to make some fundamental shifts across areas of operations, beginning with the adoption of an enterprise-wide strategy that carries us from a pure, product-obsessed approach to a more customer-focused operating practice.

To make my point, let's get grounded with where companies are today. Generally, I see three categories.

At one end of the spectrum, there are those companies whose lifeblood has been a disciplined focus on innovation and product development. These companies, such as Novartis, Intel, Sony Ericsson and General Electric, are product specialists. As long as they can sustain a steady stream of new product innovation, and that's enough to retain competitive advantage, customer engagement will be a distant second. These are the companies I call *Product Obsessed.*

At the other end of the spectrum are companies like Amazon.com, Zappos. com, Gilt Groupe and Tesco. I refer to these organizations as *Customer Committed.* Many were born of the perfect combination of customer data and innovation and use customer intimacy as a strategic lever for growth.

But most companies are not Amazon.com or Zappos.com or Tesco. Rather, they live in an in-between world and lack strategic focus—not due to poor management but because diversification is a risk-mitigation strategy. By keeping many balls in motion, they can shift strategies at will. These companies are *Operational Opportunists*, simultaneously juggling product development, innovation and customer tactics wherever needed.

They compete on efficiency or product innovation or some combination thereof. Those with data sporadically use it to solve point-in-time issues such as customer service problems, or to drive basket size, sales or other measures. Sure, customer service and targeted campaigns will always be an arrow in their quiver, but they haven't completely integrated the customer into their strategy or into how they architect their brand experience. Because of this, Operational Opportunists fall short of fully vesting themselves in using customer intimacy as their strategic lever.

Making the Loyalty Leap

Assuming a company is prepared to move customers into its business equation, what steps are we really asking it to take? It's not a somersault or a back flip, but it is at least a clear and deliberate step, or leap, to the right.

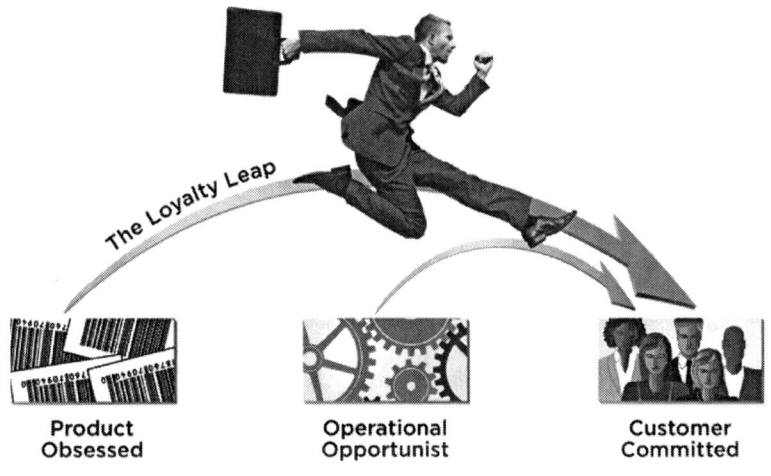

If you're an Operational Opportunist, this *Loyalty Leap* demands a more systematic and disciplined approach to the use of customer data; it takes a genuine commitment to transforming your one-way customer channels into two-way dialogue channels and thinking about product innovation and operations through the customer lens. Incorporating customer data or customer-centric strategies into your fundamental operations does not require you to tear up the strategic floorboards. Customer Commitment is just that: A commitment to making customers the heart of everything you do as a company.

If you're a Product Obsessed organization, the *Loyalty Leap* is also a step to the right, but one where design, innovation and production have had a singular focus. It's time to open up to customer data and the innovation insight it brings.

Of course, making the *Loyalty Leap* first requires embracing Enterprise Loyalty. If traditional database marketing results in direct-to-consumer communications and changing behavior, then Enterprise Loyalty extends the application of data to those thought processes that have customarily been operationally focused. Simply put, Enterprise Loyalty transitions the application of data to areas of the company that have rarely or never before used such information to guide their decisions.

To do this, you will need buy-in from your people. Employees are an indispensable source for making Enterprise Loyalty happen. If your staff is not engaged in your company, then they probably aren't going to be loyal to it. And without their loyalty, it is unlikely they'll be able to capture the interest, and hearts, of your customers.

Bryan Pearson is president and CEO of LoyaltyOne and author of

"The Loyalty Leap: Turning Customer Information Into Customer Intimacy" *and the e-book "The Loyalty Leap for B2B: Turning Customer Information Into Customer Intimacy." Follow Bryan at www.pearson4loyalty.com.*

CHAPTER 4

Loyalty Marketing: Where Are We Today?

By Tanya Bhothinard

COLLOQUY's recently-released findings from its 2013 loyalty survey estimate that membership in loyalty programs in 2012 was at an all-time high of 2.6 billion. An average HH/person is enrolled in 21.9 programs. That means roughly 119 million people are involved in loyalty programs.

This was not surprising news. We have seen this upward trend over the years. There are a number of drivers contributing to this growth in membership. From a manufacturer's perspective, it is easier and more cost effective to build a program today than at any time in history. The average cost to launch a program can range from $1 – 125 per member. On the low end, a program can be as simple as a paper-based punch card. On the other end of the spectrum are purchase-required programs with unique pin codes. These are entered on an online platform with mobile capabilities such as My Coke Rewards.

From a consumer perspective, enrolling in a loyalty program is easier than ever. Simply by entering your email and clicking a few consent boxes, a new membership can be yours in no time. To fuel this growth, brands often offer a discount; for example, an instant 10% off your purchase. With these types of promotions, it would be silly *not* to join prior to purchase. Companies such as Pottery Barn and Bed Bath & Beyond employ this strategy to capture consumer information, which they then use for promotions, enticing further purchases.

In 2013, Partners in Loyalty Marketing and the Shopper Technology Institute surveyed 100 consumer packaged goods (CPG) manufacturers about their loyalty marketing usage. Supplementing these results with our extensive knowledge in this field, we found that loyalty overall remains a balancing act for both manufacturers and consumers.

The Balancing Act

Today's loyalty programs take on many forms based on a range of criteria that include:

- Retailers vs. manufacturers

- Consortium of brands vs. individual brands

- High tech vs. low tech

- Purchase required vs. activity based

- General vs. specific strategy.

The first distinction in classifying a loyalty program is determining if it is retailer or manufacturer based. This is an important consideration for consumers: Do I personally want to engage with my primary grocery store, Meijer? Or would I like to be a member of Huggies' Enjoy the Ride Rewards? In considering this decision, I weighed the benefits of each program. Is it time consuming? How much will I likely save or gain in prizes? While I joined both, my behavior between them was very different. With Meijer's mPerks, I clipped offers and paid more attention to circular flyers. When the stars aligned, I occasionally had a coupon while the product was also on promotion. I continue to be actively engaged in mPerks – until we move and my new local store becomes Jewel.

With Huggies' Enjoy the Ride Rewards, I joined and entered my first product code the same day. (This move alone is crucial. In PILM's assessment of loyalty programs, consumers who DO NOT engage immediately – within the first day – will never engage with the program.) As our diaper needs continued, I became more attuned to pricing; that is, purchasing Pampers when we had coupons, trying Luvs, and purchasing Costco's Kirkland brand if I were making the trip. Aside from the first product code entry, I only entered one more. Three months later, I could not even recall my login name or password.

In 2009, both Sears and Starbucks launched a loyalty program. While both worked similarly, requiring a purchase to earn points for reward redemption, Sears' Shop Your Ways Rewards supported all three brands: Sears, Kmart, and Lands' End. Meanwhile, Starbucks' program worked only in their café locations. From a retailer point of view, creating a single program across its properties can be a great cost savings. Early this Fall (2013), Starbucks announced the extension of its rewards program to Teavana retail locations, as well as Starbucks coffee purchases at grocery stores.

Loyalty programs today range from high tech with mobile technology to simple punch cards. On the high technology front are programs such as Cartwheel by Target. By logging in with my Facebook account, I can access offers at Target. In addition, I can also share or post the offer as part of my Facebook updates. On the other side of the spectrum, I also have a punch card from Happy Feet, a local foot massage place. After 10 visits, I will get one free massage. While there is a vast difference in technology, both of these programs get me to come back.

A key distinction between loyalty programs is whether they are activity-based vs. purchase-required loyalty programs. In our opinion, purchase-required programs have the advantage of a guaranteed sale. My Coke Rewards, commonly cited as a leading loyalty program, is one such program. By entering codes printed on the inside of the cap, members can earn points for rewards. Contrast this with the Pepsi Pulse loyalty program. While similar in aspects to My Coke Rewards, it differs in that points are earned by doing activities and not purchases.

	My Coke Rewards	Pepsi Pulse
Free to join	✓	✓
Points / $ Earned	✓	✓
Purchase required to earn pts	✓	✗
Discounts / Coupons	✗	✗
Enewsletters	✓	✓
Other interface	App	✗

Over this past year, we have witnessed some key changes in grocery store loyalty programs. While Safeway invested more in their Just for U initiatives, Jewel, Acme, Shaw's, and Albertson's closed the door on their frequent shopper cards. Albertson's LLC stores' new approach is "Card Free Savings." From a retailer perspective, they simply were not maximizing the potential of the program. Coupled with the fact that loyalty cards are not a point of differentiation anymore, the decision makes sense.

Balancing Act for CPG Manufacturers

Loyalty programs are also a balancing act for manufacturers. In the 2013 PILM-STI summer survey, 53% of CPG manufacturers reported having a loyalty strategy in place. Among those engaged in loyalty, the top three reasons were:

1. To retain existing customers

2. To encourage purchases

3. To up-sell or cross-sell other products.

Over 90% of survey respondents believe that they generated additional revenues through their loyalty programs.

When considering loyalty programs, most manufacturers think of code-entry programs such as My Coke Rewards, Pampers Rewards, or Lean Cuisine Delicious Rewards. In our experience, loyalty programs can be more informal – "Loyalty Unplugged," if you will. These programs often have a number of consumer touch points across a variety of marketing platforms. The key is to connect the different marketing tactics and require follow up from consumers.

One simple and successful tactic we have seen are instant rebates with follow-up offers. To support the launch of a new product, a client provided an instant rebate at the point of purchase. When consumers received their rebates, they also received another offer for the product. In addition to gaining trial, the brand encouraged repeat purchase. Menards, a home improvement chain in the Midwest, employs this strategy routinely. Looking through their circular ads, there are multiple rebate offers. In addition, they occasionally offer an 11% rebate off all purchases. For consumers who claim it, the rebate arrives in the form of a store credit check.

Over the summer, I was drawn into the store for a rebate offer on bamboo cutting boards. Priced at $1.99, the rebate was $1.99 – thus, a free cutting board. I purchased the limit – two – and received my rebate of $3.98, which I later used to buy $50 worth of top soil for my garden.

Menards employs this strategy over and over again. Most recently, this Fall while I was checking out, I noticed 3 in 5 people in line had a couple of gallons of deck wash. Was I missing something? Is August the optimal time to wash our deck? Did we even need to wash our deck? Upon asking the customer behind me, I realized that there was a rebate that covered the price of the deck wash. In each of the customer's cart containing the requisite deck wash, they also had other products. Clearly this is a marketing tactic that encourages more sell.

Most every retailer today, with Walmart being a big exception, has their own loyalty or frequent shopper card. Kroger is leading the way on leveraging consumers' data to segment consumers and marketing to them uniquely. Manufacturers can use this platform to grow their business and connect to consumers.

As mentioned, Safeway is changing their loyalty program, Just for U. During the Q1 2013 conference call, Safeway CEO Steve Burd said that he expected the program to reach 6 million members by the end of the year. Members account for 45% of Safeway's sales. In addition to general coupon offers, members also receive personalized offers based on purchase history. Burd has also considered the elimination of newspaper ads, as the technology for Just for U, web and mobile grows.

As some retailers focus more on their programs, manufacturers are encouraged – and at times required – to participate in the program. We have seen clients that prosper from these partnerships when brands can incorporate their best-in-class learnings. Likewise, we have also seen brands penalized for initiatives that were not successful for the retailers.

Balancing Act for Consumers

As manufacturers are balancing their loyalty strategy, consumers also have a balancing act of their own. Think about your own memberships. Personally, I can count 15 memberships I have engaged with during the past 6 months. My memberships range from credit cards to airlines to national and local stores. In addition, there are a number of programs I am no longer engaged with; for example, Pampers Rewards, Huggies Enjoy the Ride, and IKEA Family.

This brings up an important distinction: Active or engaged membership is a more accurate measurement over membership alone. The COLLOQUY 2013 loyalty survey estimated the percent of "active" membership year over year hovers around 45% (of the 2.6 billion memberships reported). Furthermore, in our experience the percentage of "highly engaged" who are the most profitable members is even lower, hovering around 10 – 20% of all members.

Technology has also streamlined loyalty memberships for consumers. Over the past few years, we have seen the emergence of programs that link networks of brands and stores together in a consortium. There are consortium programs for online merchants such as FatWallet, MonaBar, and Ebates. These programs include a network of national brands and retailers including PetSmart, Toys "R" Us, Staples, New Egg, and Office Depot. In addition to coupons or special promotions, consumers can earn points for shopping, taking a survey, or visiting websites for rewards.

Not to be outdone by national brands and retailers, there's also a consortium for small to mid-size brick- and-mortar merchants that consumers can join. In Chicago, Belly and Five Stars are the most prominent. Other programs include Perka, Thanks Again, and Perkville. These consortiums provide the loyalty platform for small business to execute a loyalty program. By using one program, I can earn points at my local lunch restaurant, hair salon, and 7-Eleven. After meeting a point threshold, I can redeem for a free appetizer, hair products, or a Slurpee.

Lastly, from a consumer perspective, most loyalty programs are simply not unique. In comparing Pampers Rewards and Huggies Enjoy the Ride, both programs require a purchase to earn points and offer rewards for points. Both offer newsletters with parenting and baby tips. And both have apps to support the program. The only point of difference is that Huggies offers its members' coupon offers through the program, while Pampers does not. Instead, their offers are most often through the P&G BrandSavers.

In July of 2013, Office Depot debuted its loyalty program, Office Depot Rewards. Along with identical benefits, the name, logo and colors are overwhelmingly similar to Staples Rewards. While keeping up with the competition is necessary for every brand, does it drive me as a consumer more to one over the other?

	Huggies Enjoy the Ride	Pampers Rewards	Staples Rewards	Office Depot Rewards
Free to join	✓	✓	✓	✓
Points / $ Earned	✓	✓	✓	✓
Purchase required to earn pts	✓	✓	✓	✓
Discounts / Coupons	✓	✗	✓	✓
Enewsletters	✓	✓	✓	✓
Other interface	App	App	App	App

Balancing Cost vs. Rewards

While every brand and manufacturer we've encountered supports the importance of loyalty, very few are actually investing in it. In the PILM-STI loyalty survey, an overwhelming 71% of manufacturers said their investment in loyalty has increased over the past year. Even more, 87% predict that investment will continue to grow over the next three years. Yet, when asked to break down their investment in loyalty programs, 13% responded that they invest nothing. Another 56% invested a mere 1-5% of their budget to loyalty. No wonder so many believe their investment will grow!

Another misconception we often encounter is the pay-off from loyalty programs. Most programs measure success by the number of members in the program. Thus, most of the investment is spent on adding members every year. While acquisition is certainly important, the member's engagement is more telling. We have seen brands focus on acquisition, only to realize that just 20% of new members were actually engaging with the program. Most of their new members signed up and never logged in again. While some of this could be attributed to the consumer or member, part of the fault lies at the feet of manufacturer that talks me into joining and then does not speak with me again. In short, acquisition is a cost center; engagement (retention) is the profit center.

Best Practices of Loyalty Marketing

My Coke Rewards, Kroger, and Procter & Gamble are often considered the gold standards of loyalty programs. What do they have in common? In executing their program, each of these brands *segment and engage* their members. Their activities are monitored to determine usage, behavior, and purchasing profile. Using this information, a proper engagement strategy is executed. That means new members who have not engaged within the first week might get an email for free or bonus points on their next engagement. For members whose activity has declined month over month, a monthly reminder email of club benefits can re-engage them.

This theme of segment and engage was also reflected in our survey. Asked to describe the characteristics of best-in-class loyalty programs, manufactures responded:

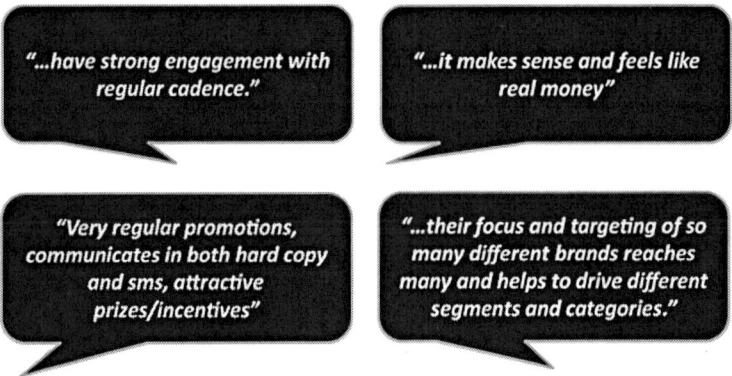

Future of Loyalty Marketing

We know loyalty will continue to be a focus. Over the years, we have seen brand's interest peak during good economic times as well as during downturns. For some brands, building a loyalty strategy during the boom years provides an edge over their competition. For other brands, the Great Recession prompted a loyalty strategy to protect and maintain their share.

While loyalty programs can be the cost of doing business as in Office Depot's case, it can also be a point of differentiation, as I saw with Menards. Loyalty programs at their best can enhance a brand's core competency. One survey responder asked, "Zappos....Do they create loyalty through their program or through providing a unique shopper experience and excellent customer service?" To answer him, it's both. A friend recently shipped a zappos.com return to diapers.com and vice versa. Both companies contacted her and rectified the mix-up. Now that's delivering on customer service to build loyalty!

Tanya Bhothinard is Senior Director at Partners in Loyalty Marketing, a Chicago-based consultancy that specializes in program strategy, optimization, and evaluation for CPG, Rx, and OTC companies. For more information: www.partnersilm.com

CHAPTER 5

Social Media and CPG Loyalty – Building Brand Communities

By Robin Newhook

For decades, marketers have been tasked with finding true pathways to customer loyalty. The interactive, personal nature of social media makes it a perfect way to promote it. But how have some consumer packaged goods (CPG) manufacturers, retailers and service providers used social media effectively? How is ROI effectiveness measured? What is the best way to embrace social media as a creative and exciting approach to connecting with consumers?

Social media is not just a passing trend; it is a vital part of any CPG's multi-channel strategy. We will look at some case studies, but first, let's discuss the relationship between social media and CPG customer loyalty.

Social media is about more than just increasing awareness and traffic to your site or platform and ultimately sales. It opens the gates to constant communication between CPGs and their consumers – not to talk *at* them, but *with* them. Social media is an interactive conversation. This personal dialogue is the key difference between social media and traditional or mass media. Social media is more about trust than selling. Consumers share their identities and express feelings via social media – and it can be an extremely personal relationship.

All humans need to find their own identity, individuality and uniqueness. But there is also comfort in being part of a group. Social media is about expressing individuality as well as being part of a larger group. In his essay, *The Sociological Imagination,* C. Wright Mills states, "Neither the life of an individual nor the history of a society can be understood without understanding both."

Before social media, the traditional brand model was a two-way relationship:

With social media, there is a relationship not just between the customer and the brand, but with other customers as well. Most importantly, the brand is at the center of the relationship:

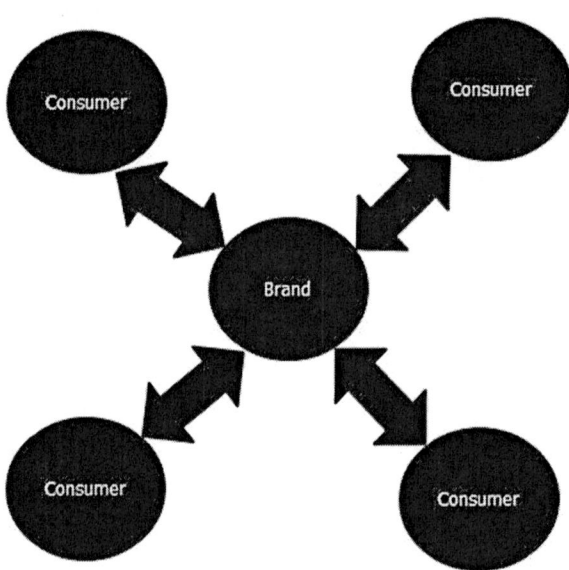

The brand being the center of the relationship defines the concept of "brand communities," which start out as psychological communities in the mind of brand users. They first identify with a brand and eventually find a connection to other people who are involved in the same activities or feelings and the role the brand plays in their lives; in other words, the social component. This attraction ultimately leads to social groupings that eventually create brand communities.

Brand communities are comprised of both psychological and social processes, underlying customer loyalty:

Psychological Components of Social Media:

- Understand what need(s) your brand fulfills in the minds of consumers; what does it stand for and mean to them.

- Use these insights gained as a strategy for developing social media platforms and promotions.

Social Components of Social Media:

- Make your social media activities "event-like" and encourage involvement; set up the conditions for a fun, playful environment. The stronger the bond the customers have to each other, the stronger the bond with your brand.

- Understand that every touch point contributes to the perception of your brand.

Here are a few case studies that demonstrate how CPG manufacturers and retailers have used the psychological and social components of brand communities through social media to build brand loyalty:

Food Lion and "Operation Grocery Drop"
The social media/brand community attribute is neighborhood pride. The program goals were:

- Generate buzz and awareness for a brand launch.

- Use digital media to share customer experiences surrounding brand launch.

How do you use social media to give credibility to a new store brand? Food Lion, the grocery chain in the southeast, had an idea: Bring free groceries right to unsuspecting consumers' doorsteps and use social media to spread the word. To launch its new value-focused private brand, My Essentials, the retailer infiltrated neighborhoods in multiple cities with entire shopping carts full of groceries. Using social media as the main driver of contests and conversations, Food Lion was able to give its customers a voice.

Food Lion leveraged social media as both a targeted and broad-based marketing channel. Facebook was used for its ability to geo-target messaging, and Twitter was used as a mass communication channel to spread messaging to the brand's entire audience.

Facebook targeted customers in three target markets in North Carolina: Raleigh, Richmond and Charlotte. Local shoppers were encouraged to "like" their Facebook page and then enter a contest telling Food Lion what made their neighborhood special. A compelling story earned them a chance to win their very own Grocery Drop. The Grocery Drop "contest" was spread organically as fans shared online photos and videos of their neighborhood and its culture in anticipation of winning their own "Grocery Drop." Food Lion then successfully brought the offline experience back to the social media, sharing the photos, videos and testimonials from these Grocery Drops.

Twitter messaging was used as a mass communication channel to spread the word about Operation Grocery Drop outside the targeted areas to Food Lion's entire customer base. Following each Drop, Food Lion hosted challenges and scavenger hunts using the hashtag #GroceryDrop. Food Lion customers across the brand were invited to participate in the #Grocery Drop conversation for a chance to win a

$100 gift card. This enabled their entire customer base – not only the winning communities – to participate and "win" as well.

ROI Metrics:

- Securing 8.2+ million media impressions and a social reach of 1.4+ million.

- Delivering 6,000 My Essentials items to about 300 homes across its three key cities.

- Earning 10,000+ unique visits to the Grocery Drop microsite housing all of the videos and photos, and receiving hundreds of posts.

Clorox Bleach and "Bleach It Away"
The social media/brand community attribute was personal experience. The program goals were:

- Leverage refreshing, humorous content as a campaign strategy to make an old brand more engaging.

- Start the dialogue within a targeted demographic, positioning Clorox Bleach as the "hero."

After nearly 100 years of establishing itself in the marketplace, Clorox Bleach sales dropped as its traditional consumers aged. The established brand was not connecting with a new, younger audience. Clorox launched its "Bleach It Away" campaign, a frank and funny program highlighting life's bleachable moments, geared to reach new parents.

Clorox learned that most of these new parents were between the ages of 25 and 35 – Generations X and Y. This demographic often turns to social media to commiserate, get advice and share stories. While they often share experiences online, it is more a statement of the event or experience rather than sharing a solution. Clorox turned these experiences into funny success stories with bleach as the solution. A variety of digital social platforms were used to show new parents how bleach could add a happy ending to their messy moments of spit-ups and dirty diapers. Soon thousands of these online stories positioned Clorox Bleach as a real-life hero.

The resulting "Bleach It Away" campaign infused Clorox Bleach into existing conversations on Twitter, online forums, Facebook, blogs, and newsletters. The campaign also enlisted 11 digital influencers who shared their bleachable moments with the audience and encouraged readers to do the same.

More importantly, bleach sales grew. The campaign contributed to the best period of volume growth for Clorox liquid bleach in more than two years. The "Bleach It Away" campaign not only stemmed declining sales, but increased talk of Clorox Bleach online by 40 percent.

They also engaged new mom and author Bethenny Frankel in an online video series of conversations to talk about messy moments involving breast milk mishaps and bathtub poop. Once again, Clorox Bleach was the "hero" for these messy moments.

ROI Metrics:

- 40% overall increase in all Clorox Bleach online conversations.

- 131% increase specifically for the "Bleach It Away campaign."

- Nearly 13 million social media impressions.

Sandwich Thins and Weight Watchers

The social media/brand community attribute was lifestyle. The program goals were:

- Encourage consumer use as part of an overall healthy lifestyle.

- Partner with prominent brand to establish credibility.

After initially branching off the Sandwich Thins community from its parent brands Arnold, Oroweat and Brownberry, a Facebook location was created for consumers to engage in a conversation with others interested in eating healthy. The Facebook page for Sandwich Thins was a great opportunity to build brand awareness, presence and likeability. A conversation was encouraged through content surrounding a healthy lifestyle that focused on Sandwich Thins as a part of that lifestyle.

Sandwich Thins further strengthened engagement with the support of a Weight Watchers endorsement, a strong brand which shared the same strategic positioning. The Facebook page housed a recipe gallery focusing strictly on the Weight Watchers recipes. Fans were able to view a display of Weight Watchers healthy creations, the PointsPlus value associated with that recipe, and share the recipe with others. Since the launch of the page and without other advertising spend, the recipe gallery received a significant increase in fans, likes, comments, and shared content.

In addition to Facebook, Sandwich Thins promoted Instagram content such as photos and customized brand images to educate "fans" about the product as well encourage participation in the conversation. They also placed emphasis on the importance customer interaction through social media. The brand engaged with consumers by creating an open forum to discuss Sandwich Thins, ask questions about the product, and provide and share ideas for recipes and overall healthy living.

ROI Metrics:

- An increase in monthly fan growth of 6,694%.

- 48% increase in the number of Facebook comments.

- 62% more consumers "Liked" the page.

- 97% consumers shared a recipe on the page, demonstrating the strength of viral marketing.

Conclusion

Food Lion's encouraging a sense of community spirit, Clorox Bleach's target market of new parents sharing "messy moments," and Sandwich Thins' use of lifestyle and partnership marketing – all were new and innovative ways to get in the hearts, minds and shopping carts of consumers.

Using social media to build brand communities and promote CPG brand loyalty:

- Tears down the wall between consumers and your brand. Retailers and manufacturers tend to focus on share of shelf when it comes to reaching consumers. Using social media to connect customers with both your brand and each other drives demand and turns "share of shelf" into "share of voice."

- Consumers' words breathe life into advertising. User-generated content makes marketing more interesting and allows CPG brands to become part of the consumer conversation without interrupting it. User-generated content is both the new focus group and the new brand loyalty marketing engine.

Invest in a social media strategy. Encourage feedback from your target audience and existing customers. Think beyond a product demo or sampling to creating CPG customer experiences. Continually generate fresh and relevant interactive content.

Using social media to build brand communities and grow brand loyalty is no longer a new media channel. It is the New Normal and an important, exciting, and creative outlet for customer engagement.

Robin Newhook is President of Newhook Marketing Solutions, which specializes in multi-channel marketing communications, new

business development, product management, strategic planning, corporate branding and process reengineering. In addition, she is an Adjunct Instructor at The College of Westchester in the Business Administration department, teaching Marketing, Consumer Behavior, Sociology, Event Planning, Service Marketing and Business Ethics. For more information: www.newhookmarketing.com.

SECTION THREE
ENGAGEMENT

CHAPTER 6

The Continuum of Shopper Engagement

By Ben Sprecher

To succeed in today's marketplace, marketers need to understand the continuum of shopper engagement.

Of course, that's not a very specific statement by itself. There are many different types of consumer engagement – attention, attitude, spending, etc. – each with its own continuum. But the continuum we'll focus on here underlies all the others; it is the continuum of the consumer's mindset.

Shopper Mindsets and How to Engage Them

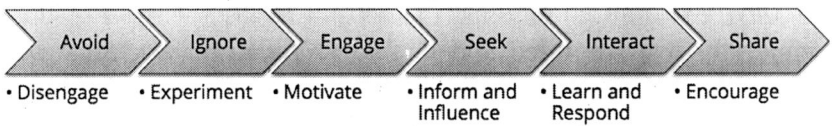

There are many different ways that a marketer can engage with shoppers, and there are many different levels of receptivity that shoppers can have. At one extreme, shoppers may be actively trying to avoid engagement, while at the other end of the spectrum, shoppers may be proactively engaging *other* shoppers on your behalf. To be effective, marketing communications need to be tailored to the current mindset of the person being reached. This requires listening to the consumer; if the marketer is just shouting a message and not paying attention, then shoppers will recoil.

The following section describes the six different mindsets that make up the continuum and discusses how to best approach shoppers in each state of mind.

Avoid: Increasingly, consumers are actively looking for ways to avoid being engaged by marketers. More than 200 million phone numbers are now registered on the National Do Not Call Registry,[3] yet there are only 115 million households in the US![4] For every 14 clicks on the content of an email, people click on the "unsubscribe" or "mark as SPAM" links once.[5]

When a person signals their desire to avoid marketing, there's only one appropriate response for a marketer: disengage quickly and respectfully. If someone doesn't want to hear from a company, then any communication will be taken negatively and will hurt the brand and any possibility of salvaging a relationship with the consumer in the future. Honor any opt-out requests and direct the resources towards more receptive prospects.

Ignore: As consumers, we are continuously barraged by a vast array of ads and marketing. Although estimates vary, the average American sees something on the order of 5,000 marketing messages a day.[6] Without an aggressive internal filter, we would become completely overwhelmed and unable to function. So, most of us simply ignore most of the marketing messages we encounter every day.

---

3   http://www.consumer.ftc.gov/articles/0108-national-do-not-call-registry
4   http://quickfacts.census.gov/qfd/states/00000.html
5   http://mailchimp.com/resources/research/email-marketing-benchmarks/
6   http://www.nytimes.com/2007/01/15/business/media/15everywhere.html?pagewanted=all&_r=0

To a marketer, this presents a significant challenge: How do you get a message to rise above the noise and get noticed? This is the time to experiment with different creative approaches, media, messages, and so forth to try to earn a shopper's attention. Most communication will fail with shoppers who are in this state of mind, so the key is variety and creativity to break through the barrier and pique the shopper's interest.

Engage: Once shoppers become engaged with a particular communication vehicle, the real substance of marketing begins. The person may be watching an ad on TV or in a video, listening to a radio spot, or reading a package, display, sign, web or mobile ad, etc., but the key here is that the marketing has actually earned a moment of shopper attention.

It's so rare that a shopper is willing to give their focus to a marketer that the job at this moment is very simple: *Avoid wasting the opportunity*. It is critical to use the few moments of engagement that you have earned (and likely paid dearly for) to motivate shopper behavior. An engaged shopper is still likely to be a passive one. To move the shopper up the engagement continuum, it's important to have *ONE* clear and concrete call to action.

Seek: When a consumer is thinking about your product, company, or category, they may begin to actively seek engagement. This seeking can take many forms. For example, consumers may be seeking product information such as nutritional facts, ingredients, or preparation instructions; social information such as reviews or recommendations; or price information such as suggested retail price, price comparison, offers, or coupons.

With consumers who are in the seeking mindset, marketers should aim to *inform and influence shopper behavior*. Each seeking shopper has a goal in mind. The marketer needs to make it easy for those consumers to achieve their goal, find what they are looking for, and quickly answer their questions and make a decision. Pushing your own message on the consumer at this point can be counterproductive; it can frustrate and delay the shopper in their search, and can push them back down the engagement funnel.

Interact: Traditional outbound marketing ends when the consumer sees an ad or seeks information for the product in question. But increasingly, marketing is evolving from a monologue into a dialogue, and shoppers are able to interact with the companies that market to them. Customer service inquiries and survey responses have always allowed for some of this two-way communication. But with the rise of social networking comments and electronic communications, more shoppers have come to expect real interaction with the businesses from which they buy.

All too often, marketers are unprepared for shoppers in this state of mind. Salesy come-ons or canned, corporate-sounding responses to genuine consumer questions or comments can dampen a happy customer's enthusiasm or inflame a dissatisfied customer's ire. When a customer actually makes the effort to reach out to a company, whether their motivation is positive or negative, it should be the marketer's job to engage with the consumer authentically and personally, and to use the exchange as an opportunity to learn from and respond to the shopper. Feedback from a consumer who cares is rare and valuable, so marketers should be prepared to jump on and capitalize from every consumer who reaches out. What we don't want to happen is to have the consumer walk away dissatisfied and move up to the last stage of the funnel and share their bad experience with other potential customers.

Share: If technology has enhanced shopper interaction, then it has radically amplified shopper sharing. Prior to the internet, social media, and mobile revolutions, shoppers who wanted to share their feelings about a company could do so through direct word-of-mouth with friends and family, or perhaps through a letter to the editor of a newspaper. Today, those same shoppers can reach hundreds, thousands, and sometimes millions of other people through blogs, email, online reviews and videos, and through the viral power of social media posts, comments, Likes, +1s, Tweets, Pins, etc.

This power in the hands of shoppers can be a significant double-edged sword. The passionate fan can trumpet your brand with more authenticity, credibility, and impact than any paid marketing ever could. But a single disgruntled customer, with a single viral story of a bad experience, can undermine the brand equity and goodwill that a company has built up over many years.

When engaging shoppers who want to share their experiences, marketers must proceed with great caution. Be sure to encourage and support your fans and followers by providing tools to make it easy for shoppers to share positive experiences, and by acknowledging and thanking them for their support. But when a shopper is sharing negative experiences, don't give them any additional ammunition to hurt you. Keep interactions positive, try to resolve issues quickly and fairly, and know when to disengage if you can't fix the situation.

Engagement Is a Means, Not an End

Despite the effort taken here to lay out the continuum of shopper engagement, it is important for marketers to remember that engagement in and of itself is not a goal. An engaged shopper who sees your ads, researches product info, interacts over social media, but still doesn't buy from you does not really help your business. The goal of all marketing must ultimately be to drive shoppers to buy from you.

Ironically, once a person becomes your customer, it's often better to have *less* shopper engagement, not more. Specifically, you want the shopper to become used to buying from you, and to do so with *less* thought and *less* engagement, so that it becomes a matter of habit.

As Charles Duhigg describes in his book *The Power of Habit: Why We Do What We Do in Life and Business*,[7] people are actually less engaged when they are in the habit cycle. For example, someone who is in the habit of driving the same route to and from work every day might tune out and miss the exit for an errand that is off their regular path. There is neurological science behind why that happens. When

---

7   http://charlesduhigg.com/the-power-of-habit/

people establish a habitual behavior, it allows their brains to disengage, not think about what they are doing, and therefore go about it without expending much energy.

So the real goal of marketers, who are used to thinking in terms of engagement and messages, should be to drive people to build habits around consuming their products or going to a particular store. Once a buying habit is established, any investment made in engaging the shopper may actually be counterproductive because it can disrupt the habit cycle.

The Mobile Disruption and the Evolving Path to Purchase
The traditional shopper marketing model of the path to purchase includes several "moments of truth": the pre-store stimulus, followed by the "First Moment of Truth" (FMOT) at the shelf when the consumer decides to buy the product, and then the "Second Moment of Truth" (SMOT) post-store when the consumer actually tests or tries the product.

The emergence of digital technologies has permanently altered the traditional path to purchase. Mobile has been especially disruptive because of the rapid, dramatic adoption of smartphones and the fact that consumers are always connected. U.S. smartphone use was up 30% in 2012 to 125 million users, while tablets have reached 50 million users.[8] And many smartphone and tablet users now sleep with their device by their bedside, so that it is the first thing they interact with every morning and the last thing they see before going to sleep at night.

These digital technologies are forever changing shoppers' path to purchase. For example:[9]

- 90% of all media interactions are screen based

---

8 ComScore Data Mine, ComScore Mobile Future in Focus, 2013.
9 The New Multi-Screen World Report, Google/Ipsos/Sterling, 2012; and Google Shopper Sciences, 2011.

- 50% of shoppers use a search engine in the path to purchase

- 25% of food and beverage sales are online or web influenced

- 22% of shoppers sought info from a retailer website in the path to purchase.

At the same time as digital is becoming more ubiquitous, traditional media is declining rapidly, undermining the tried-and-true ways that marketers have used for years to reach shoppers. For example, paid Sunday newspaper circulation has fallen to around 48 million – the same level that it was at back in the early 1960s[10] when the US population was only two-thirds of what it is today.

This explosion of the Internet and Internet-connected mobile devices has introduced a new moment in the path to purchase. This is the step between the stimulus and the FMOT that occurs pre-store or in-store when the consumer seeks information about the product. At Google, we call this new decision-making moment the Zero Moment of Truth, or ZMOT.[11]

And not only has a new step been added to the traditional path to purchase model, but research indicates that consumers are now jumping around between the pre-store stimulus, the FMOT, SMOT, and ZMOT, making the old linear, step-by-step model itself look more like a tangled airline route map.[12] What this means to marketers is that they need to have a plan for engaging shoppers using digital and mobile at every stage along the increasingly complex path to purchase and in every state of mind along the engagement continuum.

To understand how in-store shoppers are using their mobile devices, and how mobile influences the path to purchase and the size of

---

10 Newspaper Association of America, March 2013.
11 http://www.zeromomentoftruth.com/
12 Google/Shopper Sciences, Purchase Funnel Analysis, April 2012.

the market basket, Google conducted mobile in-store research.[13] The research found that 79% of smartphone owners are "smartphone shoppers," with 62% defined as standard smartphone shoppers who use a smartphone to assist in shopping at least once a month, and 17% defined as frequent smartphone shoppers who use their mobile phones in shopping at least once a week. Of smartphone shoppers, 90% use their phone for pre-shopping activities, such as finding locations, directions, hours and to make price comparisons, and 84% use their devices to help shop while in a store.

The research also found that shoppers who use their mobile device more, buy more. The median increase in basket size for health and beauty is 50%, with 40% for appliances, 34% for electronics, and 25% for household care products. Among the tasks these consumers do with their smartphones when shopping in the household care category: 58% make price comparisons, 41% find store locations and/or directions, 36% browse, 34% find promotional offers, and 32% find product information.

In-store price comparisons are the most common shopping activity across all categories studied. And in-store shoppers prefer mobile Internet sites to apps: 65% to 35%. So any mobile in-store engagement strategy should probably focus on the company's mobile website before investing in building or improving a mobile app.

Guiding Principles of Engagement

Whenever a marketer is thinking about engaging consumers, there are some core principles to consider:

- *Reach:* How many people will actually be able to see the message? Can the marketers put their message in front of all the people they want to get in front of? A shopper who can't be reached can't be engaged.

- *Relevance:* A store once promoted boneless smoked ham as

---

13   http://www.google.com/think/research-studies/mobile-in-store.html

"Delicious for Chanukah."[14] This is the wrong message, an irrelevant message, and for shoppers seeking information, it is a negatively valuable message. If marketers can get somebody's attention, and break through the 5,000 marketing messages a day that people receive, they'd better have something relevant to say to that person, or they are not going to get a second chance. The right whisper is better than the wrong shout.

Relevance matters, and often it's a question of physical location. Researchers found that a banner ad is up to 85 times more likely to be clicked when presented to somebody who is in a store sponsoring the ad versus when the *exact same ad* is presented to someone who is not in-store.[15] So physical location presents a huge opportunity in terms of relevance.

- *Trust:* Don't be creepy. Do things the right way. Don't SPAM people, because losing their trust means losing it forever. They will simply block offenders, who will never have the chance to talk to those consumers again. This is especially important with mobile devices as these are deeply personal devices. Therefore, marketers need to be careful not to abuse that intimacy.

- *Simplicity:* Simple wins. Make it easy for the shopper and the shopper will be more likely to engage. Make it complicated (for example, if there are seven steps to register for a program) and people will lose interest fast. In thinking about how to drive engagement, make sure that it is easy for the consumer to participate. Eliminate steps.

- *Measurability:* Before building out a program, ask "What is the goal?" and "What does success look like?" Establish baselines and the plan for measuring against them. If something isn't measured, it didn't happen.

---

14 Source: http://nancykayshapiro.livejournal.com/35633.html?thread=54321
15 http://www.mobilecommercedaily.com/walmart-dominates-mobile-retail-check-ins-report

In the future, the technology of engagement is going to continue to evolve. There are going to be more and more personal ways to talk to people, many of which we can't even imagine today. Yet whatever direction technology takes us, all of these principles will continue to apply. By carefully applying the above principles and by tailoring any communications to each level of shopper engagement, marketers can get the most from each shopper interaction.

Ben Sprecher is Commerce Strategy Lead with Google. For more information: www.google.com.

CHAPTER 7

Winning Shoppers with Big Data on In-Store Behavior

By Dr. Rajeev Sharma

Both retailers and consumer packaged goods (CPG) companies use an array of data sources that provide insights on different aspects of their business. Continuous sources of data include transaction data, loyalty data, and household panel data. The continuous data feed is augmented by a host of ad hoc data collection methodologies such as in-store intercepts, exit interviews, online surveys, shop-alongs, etc. aimed at answering specific questions about consumers and shoppers. Though these survey and observational methodologies help in addressing specific issues, they are based on a small sample and are dependent on the respondent as well as subjective interpretation of the researcher.

What about data on in-store shopper behavior? The store is perhaps the most important consumer touch-point for CPGs and certainly for retailers. A majority of the purchase decisions are made in-store. The proliferation of products and the media consumption habits are driving even more decisions to the in-store "moment of truth" rather than at home. It is not surprising that CPGs are allocating a greater portion of their marketing budgets to influencing these shopper decisions in-store. These budgets are marked as shopper marketing – or more broadly as trade promotions – and constitute a significant portion (upward of 60%) of the entire marketing budgets for most CPGs.

With so much marketing dollars at stake, there is an acute need for a more systematic data source to support investments in trade promotions and shopper marketing. Until recently, there was a big gap in a scalable data source on in-store shopper behavior for understanding and improving the ROI of shopper marketing and trade promotions. Recent technological advances have helped in creating a source for Big Data on in-store behavior. This allows brick-and-mortar retail businesses to finally apply analytics similar to what has now become routine in Internet retailing for winning over shoppers.

Technology for Big Data on In-Store Behavior

How can we systematically and objectively capture data on in-store behavior to fill the knowledge gap for shopper marketing? A recent technology breakthrough by VideoMining led to the development of an in-store measurement platform that fills the urgent need for Big Data on in-store behavior. The patented video analytics technologies evolved from R&D spanning over a decade through funding from government agencies such as the Department of Defense, Department of Homeland Security, and the National Science Foundation.

The in-store measurement platform enables accurate tracking of *every* shopper from the time they enter the store to the time they check out or leave the store; that is, the complete in-store path to purchase. It also extracts numerous data points on the behavior of the shoppers relative to *all* products and displays; that is, every in-store "moment of truth." The software also automatically derives the demographics (gender, age range, and ethnicity) of shoppers to help CPGs and retailers understand segment-specific shopping behavior. For example, understanding the differences between the shopping patterns of men vs. women or how different age groups respond to a specific merchandising display.

By synchronizing the time of check out, the transactional basket data is integrated with the behavioral data, along with all available information on product locations, planograms and promotions. Thus each store that is part of the VideoMining Store Panel generates a very rich set of millions of data points for each shopping trip. Automation enables capturing of data for millions of shopping trips across variations in marketing and merchandizing stimuli, creating the much needed source of Big Data on in-store behavior.

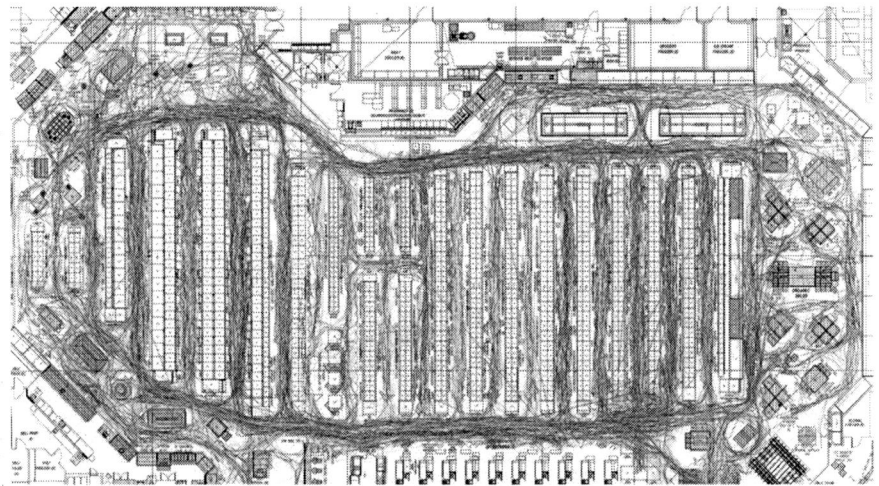

Tracking the in-store path-to-purchase for every shopper in a grocery store in VideoMining's Store Panel

Operationally, the video sensors used for measurement are ceiling mounted and non-obtrusive – just like the ubiquitous security cameras. The generation of behavioral data from video is a completely anonymous process – with no personal data ever being captured. Compared to emerging new sources of Big Data such as signals from mobile phones where individuals are identified, there are no privacy concerns because of the anonymous nature of the data. It also yields the accuracy and richness that is not available through mobile devices – for tracking the path to purchase (location) and measuring the moment of truth (or at-shelf behavior).

The central premise of this emerging Big Data technology is that "actions speak louder than words." Unlike many traditional research methods, this reveals *what shoppers actually do* – not what they say they do. This ability to capture unaided responses to the shopping environment results in an untainted perspective of shopping behavior. Most importantly, automation enables the objective gathering of data from a very large sample of shoppers, delivering reliable and representative data that is not available through traditional methods that rely on manual processing.

A Store Panel for Big Data on In-Store Behavior

To generate Big Data on in-store behavior, one approach is to create a panel of stores which can be used for capturing in-store behavior in response to different elements of the store (category layout, aisle layout, planogram, secondary displays, promotions, etc.). The panel can be representative of a retail chain or channel analogous to the household panel for consumer data. For example, VideoMining has partnered with major retailers in the convenience and grocery channel to create a representative national store panel. Establishing a store panel with generation of continuous data provides visibility into variation in shopper behavior across seasons, year-over-year trends as well as the impact of ongoing promotions. Store panel from multiple retailers also enables benchmarking of shopper behavior and key performance metrics across retailers for all categories.

Sample Metrics

With the scalable technology for measuring in-store behavior, a host of Big Data can be generated representing different groups of valuable metrics for addressing a variety of analytical questions. We discuss three groups of metrics and key questions each help in addressing. They are:

1. **Big Data on *Path-to-Purchase***

This group addresses questions related to a category or a brand's ability to attract, engage and convert shoppers into buyers, for example:

- How effective is my category or brand in converting shoppers into buyers?

- Is my promotional display getting enough exposure? How does the exposure vary by retailer?

- Where should I locate the display to produce the best incremental sales?

- Does my category adjacency help in attracting additional traffic and conversion?

- What is the walk-away rate for my category/brand?

- Is there incremental opportunity in increasing conversion rate for my category/brand?

Sample Path-to-Purchase Metrics:

- *Traffic:* Out of 100 visitors to the store, the number of people who pass a category or a display. This represents the exposure that a category or display gets.

- *Shopper:* The number of people who stop and actively interact (visually or physically) with a category or a display (out of 100 store visitors). This represents the ability of the category or a display to engage.

- *Shopper-to-Buyer Conversion*: Percentage of shoppers who became buyers. This represents the ability of the category or display to convert "interest in buying" to an actual sale.

- *Shopper Leakage:* The number of shoppers that walk away without buying after stopping to shop, and the corresponding dollars in lost sales on that trip for a category or display. This represents the loss of opportunity in converting active engagement into sales. The dollar leakage quantifies the potential total incremental opportunity in expanding sales from category/display by eliminating walk-aways.

76 | NEW DIRECTIONS IN SHOPPER TECHNOLOGY

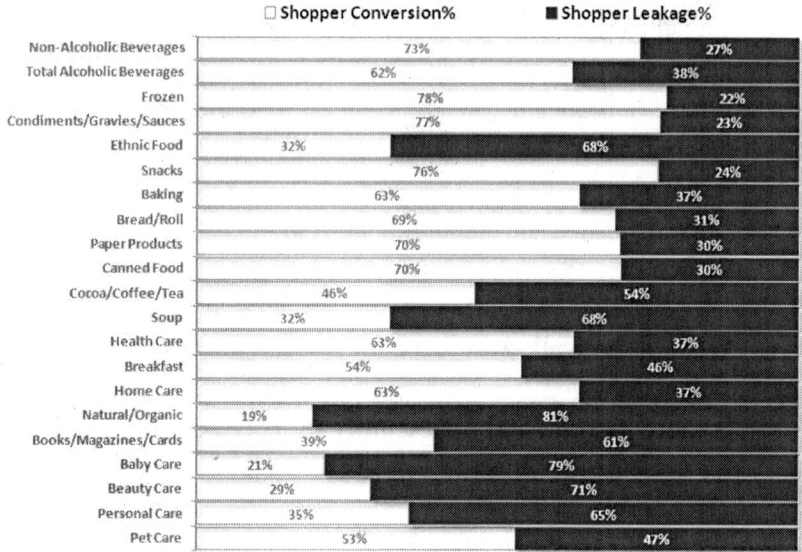

Sample benchmarking of shopper leakage metrics across Center Store departments.

2. Big Data on *Moment-of-Truth*

This group addresses questions related to the actual decision process when the shopper is front of a product category or a display. For example:

- How complex is the purchase decision process?

- How much interaction is there with product packaging?

- What visual and physical interactions are helping with the purchase decision?

- What is the behavior of people who are not buying? What could be the purchase barrier?

- How does the decision process in my category compare with other categories? At other retailers for the same category?

- How easy it is to navigate the category?

- What factors impact the shoppability of my category?

Sample Moment-of-Truth Metrics:

- ***Shopping Time:*** Average shopping time is measured by amount of time (seconds) shoppers spent interacting with a category. This represents the overall complexity of decision making. Longer shopping time does not guarantee higher conversion rate.

- ***Long-Haul Shoppers (%):*** The percentage of all shoppers in a category who take longer than 60 seconds to decide. This metric represents one of the aspects of decision complexity of the category based on shopping time.

- ***Navigation Complexity (%):*** The percentage of total time in category spent in navigating (moving around) as opposed to stopping and actively interacting with products. This metric is one of the indicators of potential navigational issues in a category.

- ***Brand Comparison Index:*** The number of brands or product types compared before making a decision. This indicates the openness of the shoppers to consider different brands in a category.

3. Big Data on Shopper-Centric Productivity

This group addresses questions related to the productivity of a category that goes beyond the traditional measures to help in focusing on the shopper and more actionable factors. For example:

- How efficient is a category in meeting shopper's needs?

- How can the category be organized to minimize any waste of precious shopping time?

- How does my category compare to others in benefitting from exposure?

- Can we make a case for greater space allocation based on relative performance?

- Should the category's growth strategy be to drive more traffic or to engage/convert more passers-by?

Sample Productivity Metrics:

- ***Time Productivity:*** Dollars sold per minute of shopper time in a category. This metric represents the return on shopper time for the category. Categories that have less time efficiency are good candidates for shelf innovation.

- ***Value of Traffic (Exposure):*** Dollars sold per patron who passes a category, or Dollar Sales/Traffic. This is the value of traffic measured by dollar revenue per category traffic. Categories that respond well to traffic are good candidates for additional space through secondary merchandising vehicles such as end caps and displays.

- ***Value of Shopper (Engagement):*** Dollars sold per patron who interacts with a category, or Dollar Sales/Number of Shoppers. This is the value of shopper measured by dollar revenue per category shopper. Categories that respond well to shoppers are good candidates for signage or other innovations such as like aisle bump-outs to capture the attention of shoppers.

There are dozens of other powerful metrics that can be generated from the in-store measurement platform. These metrics become even more useful as they are benchmarked and indexed across all categories and across a channel such as grocery or convenience. The indices also provide a sound basis for comparing the key performance characteristics of each category. The benchmarked data helps in identifying key opportunities; for example, which categories to target for increasing exposure or which categories to target for improving engagement. The data can be used as a component in space planning, promotional planning and other aspects of category management and shopper marketing.

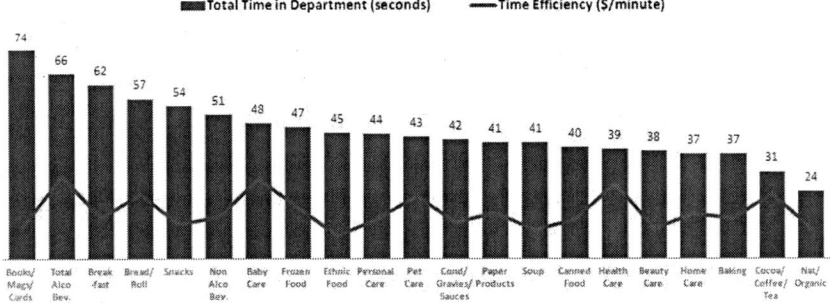

Sample benchmarking of Time Efficiency and Total Time for Grocery Departments

Big Data in Action

Applications of Big Data on in-store behavior range from simple filling of the gap of "what happened in-store" to predictive modeling and optimization of all customer-facing elements of retail. It impacts all major aspects of category management and shopper marketing. Following are two case studies representing examples of how two CPG companies – Sara Lee and PepsiCo – utilized the in-store behavior "Big Data" to their advantage. The case studies represent two disparate categories – bread and Carbonated Soft Drinks (CSD). Both were presented at industry conferences and share only the key ideas due to the proprietary nature of some of the information involved.

Let's look at the two case studies:

PepsiCo Enhances Path to Purchase

PepsiCo's goal was to increase beverage sales in convenience stores and supermarkets through a better understanding of shopper behavior. At a recent marketing conference, Kent Bassett, Senior Director of Shopper and Channel Insights for PepsiCo North America Beverages, shared how Big Data on in-store behavior from the VideoMining Panel was used effectively by them to meet that need in both the channels.

PepsiCo focused on the following three questions and developed new merchandizing strategies based on the new shopper insights:

How do Hispanics shop differently from Non-Hispanics? Extensive analysis was conducted on store-wide shopping patterns of Hispanic shoppers and their at-shelf behavior to understand the differences compared with non-Hispanic shoppers. There were a host of learnings, but the most important conclusion was that there *are* significant differences. For example, the difference was much more prominent in the convenience channel. A "heat map" there demonstrated the decidedly more goal-oriented shopping patterns from Hispanic shoppers. They spend less time in store. They buy different products, and they actually buy different "forms" of products in a category. For example, they buy fountain beverages instead of bottles and cans.

How does shopping behavior differ for different trip missions, particularly in grocery? The storewide behavior analysis of millions of trips from each trip type – pantry stocking and quick trip – revealed the differences in the shopping patterns. For example, in a pantry stock-up trip, shoppers spent a lot of time going up and down the aisles, yet the conversion rate for the beverage categories was relatively low. In fact, the more time they spent, the conversion rate fell off, which was counter-intuitive. The quick trips had a more focused "heat map." The shoppers spent significantly more time actually shopping and the conversion rate was higher. These insights were used to develop strategies for winning shoppers on pantry stocking trips.

What is the impact of location on shopping behavior and conversion rate? All key locations in the store for both grocery and convenience were analyzed to compare the impact of location. One of the key conclusions was that impulse purchases can happen anywhere. The performance varied significantly for displays at different locations in the grocery store. The performance in convenience store locations was highly dependent on the mission. Using this and other analytics, PepsiCo develop a "model store" configuration for the convenience channel and developed new display ideas such as three-sided and rounded end-caps. Many of these innovations were rolled out after testing in the same store panel to pinpoint the impact on shopper behavior.

Sara Lee Optimizes Bread Aisle

Sara Lee was a leader in fresh bakery, a category that has a prominent role in grocery. It is #3 in dollar sales and #2 in profits of all the categories. At the LEAD Marketing Conference hosted by the Shopper Technology Institute, Kyle Reynolds, then the Director of Category Management and Insights, described how Sara Lee diligently refined its bread shelf sets using Big Data on in-store behavior. It boosted sales and profits, while enhancing its reputation for providing shopper insights and effective category management.

The in-store behavior data showed that bread has one the highest shopper-to-buyer conversion rate of all the categories. This data was used in two ways. First, to establish that perimeter is a better location for bread compared to center aisle. The traffic to the category was 51% more in perimeter, which had significant impact on category performance. Second, to propose adding a bread end-cap positioned strategically next to complementary products. The in-store behavior data was used to prove that the performance of bread end-cap was at par with other leading categories and did not cannibalize sales from in-aisle sets. The bread end-cap actually led to a lift in sales of adjacent product.

This insight was used to recommend to retailers the use of bread end-cap, which until then was rarely allocated to this category. Why? It was considered a stable item on most shopping lists and a destination category.

Sara Lee used the aisle traffic patterns to develop ideal category flows and adjacencies. For example, for stores with bread in the center aisle, the data showed that 71% of shoppers entered the aisle from the back of the store, with most making a U-turn to exit from the same side. This led to developing new shelf sets where frequently purchased products such as white bread were placed in the center rather than at the start of the aisle. Secondary segments like bagels, English muffins, buns and premium products were placed in the "book ends" on either side to increase exposure to these higher margin products.

The "moment of truth" data for the category helped Sara Lee establish shelf sets that were matched to the way shoppers make bread purchase decisions. For example, the bread aisle has been traditionally organized as "vendor set" which, the behavior data showed, is confusing to the shoppers compared to a "type set." There was a remarkable difference in sales performance for the two sets. Using this data, Sara Lee developed a very well received category plan for retailers called "Organize, Optimize and Innovate," which had many components including signage for helping shoppers navigate the sub-categories such as buns or muffins.

As a result of this work, Sara Lee moved steadily up the Kantar Retail PowerRanking for consumer/shopper insights and category management (based on a survey of retailers), jumping from 16th place in 2009 to 8th place in 2010.

In a Nutshell

Brick-and-mortar retail businesses have lagged behind in the use of Big Data for understanding and impacting shopper. There is an increasingly urgent need to understand and improve the ROI of shopper marketing and trade promotion spending. An in-store measurement platform and store panel fills the Big Data gap to help CPGs and retailers win over shoppers by optimizing the shelf as well as promotions. The case studies from Sara Lee and PepsiCo illustrate how Big Data in-store behavior can be applied for specific analytics for winning shoppers.

Big Data is here to stay. Both retailers and CPGs need to expand their capabilities to handle the new in-store behavior data and incorporate it into their business processes.

Dr. Rajeev Sharma is the Founder and CEO of VideoMining, a leading provider of shopper marketing insights using technology-based in-store measurement and analytics. For more information: www.videomining.com.

CHAPTER 8

An Innovation Lens for Retailer Competitive Advantage: Grocery Shopping Apps and m-Assisted Retailing

By Nancy M. Childs, PhD.

Today's reach of mobile smartphone technology and the personal and commercial blend of social media networks permit instantaneous consumer interactivity on grocery products, pricing and information access. This potential for consumers to access information, savings, and convenience through a mobile app enables a dramatic transformation in food shopping on a global basis. A revolution well underway and continually morphing, new grocery shopping behaviors represent both a challenge to comprehend and an opportunity to manage for increasing revenue and competitive advantage. Understanding consumer grocery shopping behavior in the mobile age requires fresh approaches to defining the consumer's grocery shopping experience, motivation, and value equation.

Sophisticated understanding of food culture occasions, purchase occasions, and retail provision of experience are critical to succeeding and retaining today's consumers[16]. Their interface with technology, enabling the purchase occasion, is the logical facilitator for integrating their product needs, desire to economize, and search for experience appropriate to their purchase situation.

The above recounts the evolution of digital media and grocery shopping during the past year. Research investigations and consultant prognostications are proliferating, and consumer digital behavior is both advancing and clarifying. The Peck Fellowship challenge is an exceptionally broad topic exploring an area of accelerating technological innovation across changing consumer behaviors and demographics (The Peck Fellow Year 1 Research Report: *Digital Grocery Commerce: Exploring the Potential for Grocery Shopping Apps, 2013).*

Overview of Digital Grocery Shopping

As of May 2013, nearly 60% of American adults and nearly 40% of teens have a telephone operating on a smartphone platform[17], and smartphone penetration is accelerating at a linear 10% annually for several years. Consumers using smartphones can no longer be characterized as innovators and early adopters as they've quickly penetrated into the late majority space.

A year ago, consumers reported the excitement of mobile was driven by the convenience and connectivity. The access to apps, internet and email was seen among the top advantage to owning a smartphone. Least liked, in 2012, were the phone's intrusive interruptions, billing, and the mechanical difficulties of battery life, dropped calls, signals and such difficulties.

Data developed by Booz & Company for the Food Marketing Institute (FMI) report almost as many shoppers are using their mobile while shopping (31%) as shoppers using online coupons (32%). A powerful potential in grocery app development for smartphones is the

---

16 FMI 2012, "Challenging Consumer Financial Realities = In-Store Opportunities", Harvey Hartman, The Hartman Group, April 2012.

17 A. Smith, Smartphone Ownership Update – 2013, Pew Research Center, June 5, 2013.

consumer's natural desire to use the smartphone to serve as a multimedia digital communication device, through texts, tweets, email, instagram, and a multitude of social media sites. This ability to digitally connect and create exchange between the consumer and retailer, and consumer to consumer, is powerful. The smartphone is the natural location for the digital discussion.

Insights: Digital connection with the shopper via the app is sensitive. An important set point exists for each consumer between their desired level of interchange and annoyance. Allowing each consumer to establish this comfort point is important, as is devising receptive ways to strengthen the consumer's need for the depth and frequency of this interchange via the app. The consumer needs to feel in control.

An appealing aspect to the retailer in grocery app development is that the consumer provides the hardware – their smartphones – and that it is the consumer's desire and routine to be engaged with the phone as they shop. It also is an inherent disadvantage in that some respondents find having to view the screen of a handheld device while shopping (unlike Bluetooth conversation with the smartphone in the pocket) is awkward and perhaps unsafe. The screen is small and many are concerned about smartphone theft.

Insights: Concerns over hardware/software performance remain a dilemma. As grocery apps are developed in the future, issues of platform, signal, and multiple concerns of coordinated hardware and software across multiple devices will continue to hinder the achievement of consumer expectations. Consumers are unforgiving when an app disappoints. This area will remain a challenge in shopper acceptance of grocery apps. The smartphone is both an information asset and a physical inconvenience during the manual act of grocery shopping. The screen is small and consumers fear smartphone theft if it is left unattended.

Penetration of e-Commerce in Grocery Shopping

Grocery shopping is one of the consumer's most frequent and

ingrained retail shopping habits. Despite extensive study and thoughtful intervention, the consumer's path to purchase remains difficult to influence. From early years of observing mom's shopping habits through establishing one's own household and accompanying responsibilities, consumers become ingrained in a pattern of sales circular review, price comparison, and familiarity with a limited set of products, brands, retailers, and recipes that are relied upon for feeding and satisfying their family. Coupons remain an important part of their behavior. Channel blurring cannibalizes grocery fill-in and stock-up shopping, but for the majority of shoppers, major trips remain relatively unchanged.

Information seeking, recipe access, and coupon search behaviors show the most change. Consumers have tended over the years to expand the role of foodservice and take-out to fulfill their family's meal needs rather than to alter their routine grocery shopping behavior in significant ways. While their change in grocery shopping behavior is slow, especially in established households, it is occurring.

The social and digital world vastly expands the variety and ease of engaging the consumers' involvement in food. The evolution in grocery shopping behavior is slower, on the edges of majority behavior. It is more significant in smaller consumer segments, and driven by special need situations. The Hartman Group deconstructs digital involvement with food into the four phases of meal planning, shopping, preparing, and eating.[18] Each stage is a separate opportunity to engage the shopper's food experience strategically through social media and m-assisted shopping. The Hartman Group research indicates grocery opportunities lie more with recognizing that grocery shopping behavior is dominated by browsing (66%) rather than search and retrieve (32%). The consumer's desire to be engaged in food selection, especially the increasingly important fresh and prepared categories, challenges the grocery online shopping model.

---

18 Harvey Hartman, "The Online Grocery Opportunity", The Hartman Group, 2012.

In March 2012, The Hartman Group reported 57% of consumers sought a relationship with their primary grocery store, and more importantly, the vast majority wanted the store to communicate with them online via email (66%), Facebook (17%), corporate website (17%), or text (7%.)[19] A year later, NGA/Bricks Meets Clicks research with grocery shoppers from seven retail banners echoed these shopper desires. The research reported connection with their retailer by website (average 68% of shoppers), email (53% average), and Facebook (20% average).[20]

Insights: *The retailer's opportunity is building communication and relationship via digital to sustain the in-store experience rather than eliminating the in-store experience with digital commerce. The quality and purpose of the digital conversation becomes critical, demanding relevance and interchange. It is not an "on-sale" push model that provides information already available in the retailer's traditional media. Grocery smartphone apps need to deliver added benefit, perceptually and in execution, at strategically selected phases of a meal's development (planning, shopping, preparing, eating). Recognizing the most desired app functions, the meal phase they impact, and addressing app barriers are critical for retailer success.*

The inertia hindering change in grocery shopping is one of the reasons that online grocery shopping has one of the lowest penetrations of e-commerce among retail categories. McKinsey & Company research indicates 95% of consumers report that their last grocery purchase was made in the store, that only 1% was online, and that the remaining 4% purchased in other locations, likely boutiques and the growing farmer's market channel.[21] As research from PricewaterhouseCoopers (PwC) shows, as recently as 6 months ago, nearly 90% of grocery shoppers still prefer to shop in store, and most prefer to do so without involving online research.

---

19 The Hartman Group, Shopper Topography, 2012.
20 NGA/Brick Meets Click, Shoppers are Ready for Digital Connections with Their Food Retailers, Digital Check-up for Grocery, 2013
21 P. Dazell-Payne, J. Liebowitz, and K. Roche, How is the American online consumer evolving?, Consumer & Shopper Insights, McKinsey&Company, September 2012.

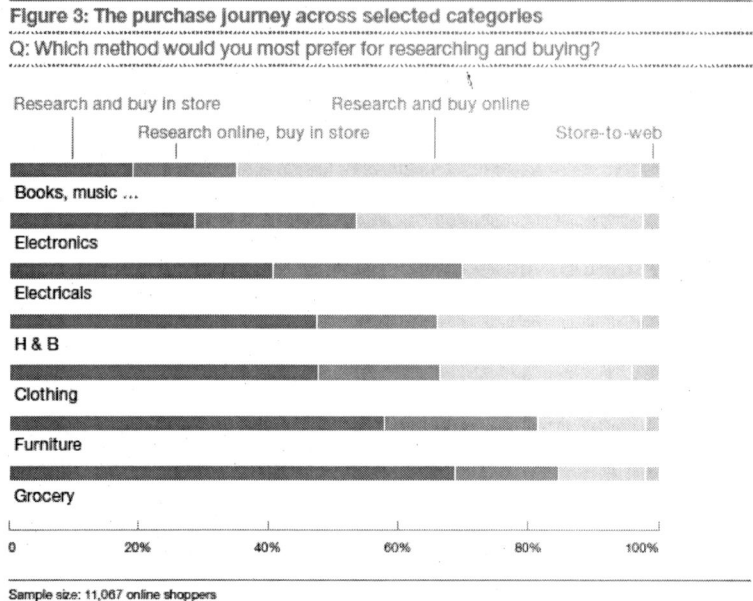

Source: PwC, 2013[22]

McKinsey & Company concludes that the grocery channel, relative to other channels, is an online e-commerce laggard and not likely to be in the "digital battleground" in the near future. They also do not see significant differences in online purchase by age in the grocery category.[23] The NGA/Brick Meets Click 2013 research reports that 10-16% of shoppers from seven selected grocery banners bought some groceries online in the past 30 days.[24]

Low grocery online shopping is somewhat surprising given the advancing penetration of smartphones and the wide experience consumers have with general online shopping. Peck qualitative research confirms the shopper's reticence to shop online for groceries. Their grocery shopping ritual is habitual and tends towards experiential as it

---

22 Demystifying the Online Shopper, PWC, 2013
23 P. Dazell-Payne, J. Liebowitz, and K. Roche, How is the American online consumer evolving?, Consumer & Shopper Insights, McKinsey&Company, September 2012.
24 NGA/Brick Meets Click, Shoppers are Ready for Digital Connections with Their Food Retailers, Digital Check-up for Grocery, 2013

is prone to browsing and not search behavior. Grocery stores are ubiquitous. Price-saving opportunities at grocery are not as prevalent or substantial as other online categories with larger margins to discount. Online grocery savings often are erased by delivery costs. While online is useful for shoppers with specific circumstances, it is not yet a broadly attractive model.

Insights: *In general shoppers are savvy about the "full cost" of shopping and do not perceive enormous value saved with online grocery shopping. Without specific needs for convenience, or lack of transportation, they do not perceive a high value ratio with grocery online. U.S. grocery stores are ubiquitous. Their prices are competitive and do not result in compelling opportunities overall for digital savings. Online grocery shopping will increase, but m-assisted shopping behavior will dominate.*

Innovation, Smartphones, and Grocery Apps for m-Assisted Retailing

The current and expanding characteristics of the grocery digital commerce situation may be framed by Clayton Christensen's chart (on the next page) depicting disruptive innovation. The multitude of current and anticipated mobile apps, e-commerce, and m-commerce formats are sustaining innovations (top solid line). Most grocery app functions can be described as "sustaining" or "evolutionary innovation" with a command-and-control interface offering familiar and obvious benefits of information, convenience, and savings. This is in contrast to a more organic disruptive innovation (changes in shopping channel access; anticipatory, fuzzy logic, and artificial intelligence applications which suggest individual needs and likes)[25] depicted as the bottom solid line.

The sustaining technologies, characteristic of many grocery app functions, may be out running the general consumers' interest in utilizing them (dotted line), much like the current reticent consumer reception of QR codes.

---

25 McKinsey&Company, The Impact of Disruptive Technology: A Conversation with Eric Schmidt, 2013.

92 | NEW DIRECTIONS IN SHOPPER TECHNOLOGY

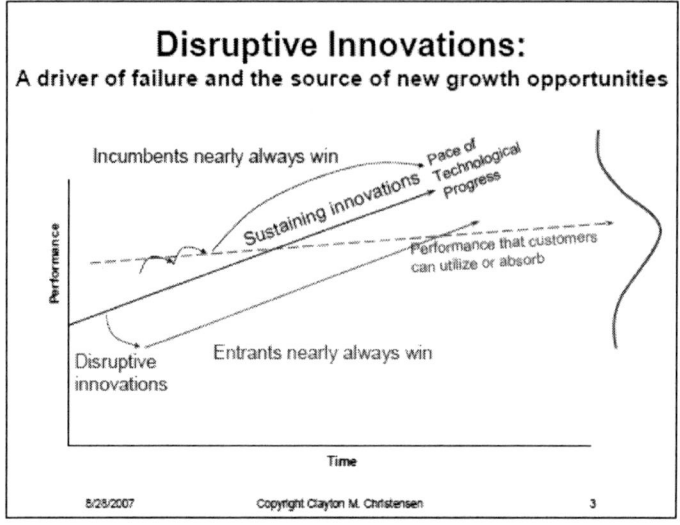

Source: C. Christensen[26]

Peck sponsored qualitative research in May 2013 with grocery consumers who were aware of but not using grocery shopping apps indicated there are several perceptual and mechanical deterrents to their engaging in digital commerce at grocery. For younger and tech savvy e-commerce shoppers, the grocery app benefit model was insufficient to entice use. Their smaller household and limited grocery basket did not generate an economic or convenience rationale that superseded their perceived cost of using the app.

An investigation of various functions for grocery apps identifies those apps that might be more sustaining innovations for grocery shoppers, thereby supporting the likelihood of the incumbent's (for example, retailer) success. Such apps include economic advantages such as exclusive discounts, price comparisons, identifying sale items; convenience advantages such as creating shopping lists, locating products, providing nutrition information; and personalization such as recalling past shopping history, and specific dietary recommendations.

---

26 Disruptive innovation, sourced http://www.claytonchristensen.com/key-concepts/ June 2013.

Disruptive Innovation and Grocery Shopping Apps

A primary interest is the emergence of new "disruptive innovation" approaches to shopping the center of the store (bottom solid line) – what they are and who is utilizing them. These disruptive innovations are likely to come from out of industry and are as likely to be championed by brand manufacturers and other channel players as by grocery retailers. Such disruptions are also the consequence of changing consumer behavior in another independent realm. For example, millennials' strong embracing of sustainability is exhibited in a growing number of lifestyle changes including less driving, more use of public transit, and less physical commuting overall. This behavior change can have profound impact on their grocery shopping behaviors, as well as their reception of new grocery shopping models.

New disruptive technologies may or may not be in the form of transformative app uses, and may engage new retail channels such as imagined by AmazonFresh's market entry. But they are enhanced by intelligent recommendations derived from consumer online searches, restaurants frequented, and from the universe of their shopping purchases. To date, disintermediation of grocery shopping is relatively minor and characterized by higher value, bulky, non-perishable, high usage categories such as diapers, paper towels, and such non-food items characteristic of a price- and convenience-driven model.

In Accenture's chart (on the next page), smartphone penetration of 58% reported by the Pew Research Center in May 2013 is now entering the late majority phase of adoption and offering incremental innovation. With smartphone penetration at this level, the environment is well prepared for the universe of grocery shoppers to accept sustaining innovations provided through grocery apps.

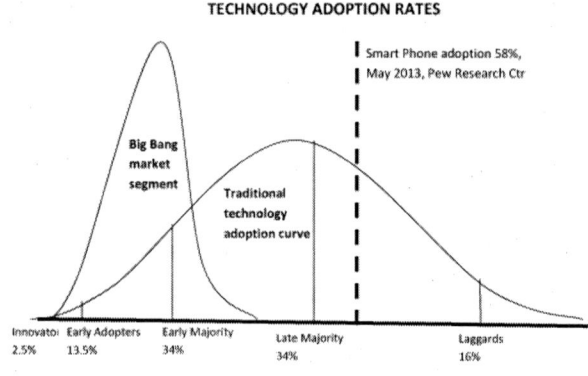

[27] Source: Accenture, 2013.

Accenture argues today's IT based "big bang" disruption leverages information, moves quickly, and provides exceptional "customer intimacy" based on one's own personal data, thereby creating a dramatic individual value proposition. At present, the retailer – and more broadly, consumer financial intermediaries – hold the consumers' retail purchase data. Sophisticated grocery app-loyalty card linkage has the potential to influence, rather than simply enable, easier shopping based only on information and digitized convenience. More importantly, this type of interactive platform enables extensive communication and learning opportunities with the retailer and within the retailer's shopper community to integrate and share, create, review, and suggest ideas between shoppers, and with the retailer. When done well, this approach generates a feedback loop for incremental improvement and innovation.

M-assisted shopping, through smartphone grocery apps, has the potential to move through tiers of functionality from information provision and shopper convenience to more interactive, personalized and anticipatory capabilities, including a dimension of gamification and entertainment. The dilemma is grocery shopping is not occasional

---

27 P. Nunes and L. Downes, Big Bang Disruption: The Innovator's Disaster, Accenture, 2013.

or inconsequential. It is an ingrained, routine, essential, and frequent behavior, and of meaningful size in the household's budget. It's a necessary endeavor and not limited to just the earliest innovators and adopters. The "big bang" innovation model advocating a quick in-and-out market approach - drop, run, and move on – minimizing quality control and support and relying on beta launches with user sourced innovation creates a dilemma in satisfying and keeping loyal grocery shoppers.

Sustaining Innovation and Grocery Shopping Apps

As grocery app users indicated in qualitative research, they require assurance of ease of use and a tangible value proposition. A sustaining innovation approach utilized by grocery retailers is appropriate given that smartphone users are now entering the late majority stage, and their habitual and tactile nature of food and grocery shopping. The Peck Research Panel of industry experts identified that grocery apps "provide exclusive discounts to app users," the ability to "track loyalty points and incentive programs," and proactive "identification of coupons and sales offers" as the most important grocery app functions for shoppers in the next eighteen months. Performance issues of most concern in the future are excessive surveys and inquiries generated by the app, "slow signal response time in the store environment," and "app glitches and cumbersome app navigation."

Sustainable innovation favors the incumbent, but only if the innovations remain relevant and useful to the consumer and avoid overwhelming the consumer with an esoteric and confusing proliferation of operations. Their performance must be easy and impactful, or disruptive innovation gains with an advantage of simplification. With all their promise, grocery apps need to be thoughtfully studied, prepared, and presented for sustainable success with grocery shoppers.

Concluding Insight: *Grocery apps are sustainable innovations which benefit the incumbent (the retailer) for competitive advantage and growth. Such apps succeed when they keep pace with consumers for relevance and desired performance.*

Nancy Childs, PhD. is a Professor of Food Marketing and a Gerald E. Peck Fellow at the Haub School of Business, Saint Joseph's University in Philadelphia. She can be reached at nchilds@sju.edu. For more information: www.sju.edu.

Source

The Gerald E. Peck Fellowship research for 2012-2015 is supported by the Academy of Food Marketing at Saint Joseph's University and by FMI. This chapter is excerpted from the Peck Fellow Year 1 Research Report: *Digital Grocery Commerce: Exploring the Potential for Grocery Shopping Apps*, 2013.

CHAPTER 9

Elevating the Voice of the Customer to Increase Decision-Making Confidence

By Ellie Hutton

The world is evolving at a pace that is difficult for marketers and insight gatherers to keep up with. Businesses need real-time insights to improve decision making confidence.

Here are a few examples of companies that could have benefited from real-time insights and a closer connection to the voice of their customers:

- A national chain of stores revamped its growth strategy to attract new shoppers, but instead ended up alienating its core consumers.

- A CPG manufacturer changed the packaging of its core product, only to cause confusion at-shelf and an erosion of brand equity.

- A national retailer re-thinking its category management practices inadvertently lost shoppers that tended to buy certain niche products.

- A media distribution company changed its consumer pricing policy without any consultation and saw huge financial losses and erosion of brand trust.

- Menu items at QSR chains failed because management made a decision on gut versus customer needs.

Insight teams can sometimes get too focused on the tactical execution of projects to answer internal stakeholder's information needs. As a result, the team may not have a good handle on the big picture for the organization, and ends up being reactive rather than proactive in approaches to answering the big questions. This means the team completes each request, but in the process does not advance their careers or the insight team's influence within the organization, or the industry. The end result is that this does not increase the decision-making confidence in more areas of the business.

We can do more, and we can do better. Marketing and insight teams need to stretch their legs to make connections with other teams in the organization. And they need to stretch their minds to get out of the rut and try new approaches to gathering insight that build engagement and customer loyalty, not break them down.

Here are some trends that marketing and insight teams can help address and find solutions to by stretching their legs and minds:

- ***The Big Data Deluge: How do you help make sense of it all?*** Gathering transactional and behavioral data isn't a problem, but figuring out the stories and insights buried within typically rates somewhere between overwhelming and impossible. The marketing and insight teams often aren't the ones responsible for steering this ship. But they do have a role to play in interpreting this information.

- ***Social Media Revolution: What's your role in the conversation?*** Figuring out the right voice and time to join the conversation is critical to the shopper relationship and both the marketing and insight team can play a role here, as well as improve the signal-to-noise ratio. Again, the marketing and insight teams are often not the teams responsible for managing social media listening or interaction. So building bridges is important.

- ***Building Lifetime Value, Engagement, and Advocacy: What is the impact of market research?*** Marketers want to have richer and deeper relationships with shoppers. If brands continuously bombard them with long and tedious surveys, it hinders this goal and does not build a positive corporate character. Insight gatherers should build on the long history of respecting the consumer in data collection methods to do more to build engagement.

- ***Measuring Return on Investment: How can you calculate dollar savings in research approaches?*** It is very easy to calculate cost savings in research approaches if you can find faster and cheaper ways of gathering insight. Proving your worth through ROI savings when it comes to research dollars spent can help elevate both the marketing and insights team in the organization.

If you are able to find solutions to some or all of these challenges then the voice of the customer will be more likely to have a seat at the table going forward. Elevating voice of the customer and shopper in the organization to influence larger, strategic decisions, as well as the smaller ones, is entirely possible if you learn to look more at the big picture and take a proactive approach to answering information needs.

Innovative companies use communities of consent or insight communities as a new insight gathering approach to address these challenges and elevate the voice of the customer and the marketing and insight teams in the organization.

Communities of Consent

For thousands of organizations, insight communities play a vital role in bringing the customer into the heart of the organization in cost-effective and impactful ways. Because your community is "always on," it becomes integral to the way you harness the voice of the customer in your business. The GreenBook Research Industry Trends REPORT – Spring 2012, shows that insight communities are the top emerging methodology used by client-side researchers — with 36% currently leveraging them.[1]

An insight community is an ongoing conversation, a relationship between you and your customers. Insights build over time, as you and your customers take part in a journey. The design of the community means you have access to the profiled information, the answers to every question ever asked, and the transcripts of every conversation. As you learn more about the people in your community, your questions become more precise and targeted, and the depth of the insights generated becomes richer.

An insight community…

- Is a private, online group of customers, prospects, employees, or other target audiences that help you get to the heart of what people think and feel, and why they do the things they do.

- Can be local or global, targeted or broad, short-term or long-term, and can include hundreds, thousands or even millions of people.

- Is for CMOs, Insight Professionals, Market Researchers, product delivery teams, and anyone who wants to gain deep insight from their customers and prospects while building a relationship.

- Is used for co-creation, innovation, exploratory, testing and validation work.

- Adds richness and validation to Big Data, and helps you be wiser about your "whys" and "what ifs" – something that data struggles to do on its own.

- Connects the voice of the customer to the heart of the organization, tapping into the minds and hearts of your customers and turning them into a source of sustainable competitive advantage.

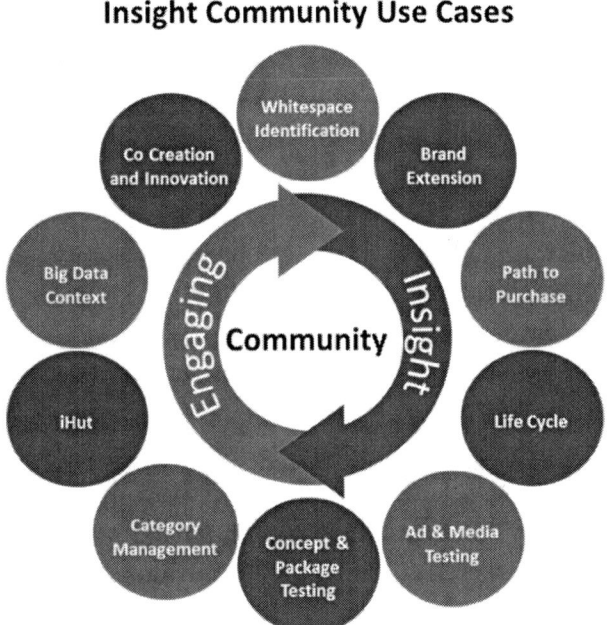

Just imagine what you could do if you had real-time, on-demand access to your key customers for all of these use cases and more. These are just a few of the ways businesses use insight communities.

An insight community helps you get closer to your customers than you have been before. It inspires customers to voice their opinions, give feedback, and feel responsible for the products they consume and the services they use. It invites them to have a closer relationship, spend more time thinking about your brand, and work with you to continuously co-create and come up with ideas that can build your competitive edge in the market. An insight community invites customers to criticize constructively and be a part of customer democracy.

Obviously, to elevate yourself and your team in the organization you need to go beyond delivering insights. Implications and recommendations need to go along with the insights, otherwise the powers that be may still be "lost in the woods" and buried in information they aren't sure how to make actionable.

The Big Data Deluge: How Do You Help Make Sense of It All?
Technology provides organizations with an enormous amount of data. IBM estimated that "90% of all the data in the world today was created in the last two years."[2]

Gathering this data isn't a problem, but the sheer volume is staggering. Also, the tools to integrate and talk to your other systems are often cost prohibitive. Companies that are beginning to make sense of it all and tie systems together are also able to do powerful predictive modeling.

Behavioral and transactional data can tell you what people are doing, and helps you schedule production, distribution, and capacity, manage inventory, and customize communications if you can build sound models. However, counting the "what" does not tell you enough about "why" a brand is chosen, why an offer is not selected, what would happen if a different scenario was offered, or why people do what they do. Traditionally, the "why" questions have been addressed via one-off surveys, focus groups, and "meet the customer" sessions. However, these have tended to be too slow, too expensive, and not sufficiently insightful.

Finding the stories and insights buried in the data, validating models, and digging into the "why" is something the Insights team can help with because they have direct access to the voice of the customer.

All you need to do is find an approach that will yield faster and cost effective results. Many companies find this solution in an ongoing, online, private insight community. These insight communities are typically built for one brand and accessed across the organization for a direct channel to your target audience.

To get in the game you'll need to build relationships with the teams who own the responsibility of the Big Data now – typically owned by the CTO or CIO. If you think about all of the data you have about the market place as an insight ecosystem, then it makes sense for you to have some skin in the game when it comes to Big Data. Showcase what you can do for them and show how you can add value to the work they're producing. This is a win-win for you, them and your business.

Social Media Revolution: What's Your Role in the Conversation?

Social media is another contributor to the Big Data conundrum, but it usually isn't owned by the same teams as behavioral and transactional data. Social media listening and interaction may be owned by PR, communications, customer care, or legacy call center teams.

Data from social media gets you closer to the voice of the customer, and tells you what people are saying about you. However, it is still aggregating on a large scale, and systems make assumptions about who you are based on what you search. It's also hard to know how you should react to a social media conversation trend. We're still in the Stone Age when it comes to plugging the social web into other Big Data stories. This is a great area for experimentation. Innovative companies are at least starting to figure out how to chart this unknown.

The trick is having access to a tool that can get you real time insights so you can determine whether you need to respond, what your voice should be, and how you should respond in hours, not days. In companies that have well-connected listening posts and that share themes and trends seen in the social media space across teams, an insight community can help determine what the reaction strategy should be as trends arise. Members of an insight community are well-profiled and trusted advisors, typically comprised of very engaged customers. Their opinion helps to determine the real signals in the noise.

You can work with your insight community to explore and validate themes you're seeing in social media and to strategize on the best reaction approach over the course of hours so you can respond in a timely fashion. Figuring out the right voice and time to join the conversation is critical to the shopper relationship and both the marketing and insight teams can play a role here, as well as in improving the signal to noise ratio.

Building Lifetime Value, Engagement, and Advocacy: What Is the Impact of Market Research?

One of the main goals of the CMO is to build brand engagement. Unfortunately, we live in a time when it has never been easier for the consumer to disengage. Consumers habitually filter out brand noise; brands can no longer just fight for attention by increasing ad budgets. The growing engagement challenge demands innovative thinking and building stronger relationships until customers turn into trusted brand advisors and ambassadors who then become the voice behind your brand, products and services.

Diffusing customer centricity throughout an organization helps build brand uniqueness that can result in a strong competitive edge. Getting closer to your customers to understand their motivation in consuming your brand, and engaging them to share their genuine feedback is an important piece of customer-centric thinking. The new battleground is in being the most customer-centric brand or organization in your market. Everyone wants to increase customer engagement to drive loyalty and retention.

When companies continuously bombard shoppers with long and tedious surveys, this does not build engagement or a positive corporate character. Insight gatherers have a long history of respecting the customer in data collection methods. Companies should take advantage of this position at a time when people are increasingly wary about the information companies hold on them. Acknowledging this helps build lifetime value, engagement and advocacy, and supports the bigger corporate goal of engagement.

Insight professionals need to go beyond the base of respecting privacy when designing projects. Companies need to consider the people who participate as people, not just "respondents." Design should be more engaging and intuitive and the tone needs to be more conversational.

It is also really important to consider the research process as a circle, not something linear with a clearly defined beginning and end point. One of the biggest frustrations consumers have with the process is the lack of follow up; they took the time out of their busy schedules to share their opinion, but typically companies don't close the feedback loop with them after the fact. In a community, sharing back is the most important motivation for participation. But there's no reason why you couldn't share back after an ad hoc project either. It only takes a few minutes to write up a thank you and a few bullets on your next steps.

Something else to consider is that free and fast online research tools have placed the ability for direct customer interaction in the hands of too many. This creates fragmented relationships which do not give organizations a holistic picture of their customer. The result is brand disengagement. In the absence of an ongoing relationship and mutual trust, it is much harder to engage customers and to inspire them to provide meaningful feedback. The marketing and insight teams need to get a handle on this and rein it in.

Building an insight community where you place the control in the hands of a few within your organization, and then nurturing an ongoing relationship built on mutual trust and respect with your customers helps you step away from fragmented relationships. This in turn will positively impact your corporate character.

Today's consumer actively engages with brands. They are willing to opt in to influence brands they care about; crowd sourcing, co-creating, and "me helping we" have taken off. Those who are closest to a brand are frequently the most critical of ideas because they have a vested interest in the business decisions soon to be made. These customers then become more than respondents. They become lifelong trusted brand advisors.

The insights team can help support customer centricity at a higher level by putting the marketing team and others in the organization in direct contact with the voice of the customer and market.

Measuring Return on Investment: How Can You at Least Calculate Dollar Savings in Our Research Approaches?

To become more competitive and to future-proof your decisions, you need to invest in understanding your customer on an ongoing basis. The most cost effective and fast way to connect is through an insight community.

Determining an ROI calculation based on the insights you convert into actions is challenging. However, it is very easy to calculate cost savings in research approaches if you can find faster and cheaper ways of gathering insight. The best way to do this is to measure equivalency; that is, how much would it cost to run the same project if you had to pay for a sample and an external vendor to execute the project. If you run a project in-house on your insight community, you'll likely see cost savings of 10-20 times. If you outsource research design through to reporting to a vendor, the savings will be about 3 times.

One of Australia's leading consumer experts documented examples of clients who have seen great ROI:[3]

- A CPG company conducts 50+ research studies on their insight community, with a conservative estimated equivalency value of $1,000,000. Actual cost was less than $250,000.

- A CPG client uses their community to conduct in-home product tests with customers at a tenth of the cost of traditional recruitment.

- Online forums replace focus groups in half the time, five times the geographic coverage, and one-tenth the cost.

- Media companies do over 250 short ad tests per annum for the annual cost of $80,000 with their own team managing it and creating norms.

- CPG companies conduct in-store shopper studies using their communities and don't have to constantly pay the cost of external sample. They simply can do twice the amount of studies so more categories or more planograms get a chance to be evaluated.

There is also a benefit beyond dollar savings. Insight communities allow clients to connect with customers more often, which means more issues and more new products can now receive input from consumers prior to launch.

Proving ROI of your research spend can go a long way to ensuring your budget gets renewed for the next fiscal, and for proving your worth within the organization. When you layer this along with all of the amazing insights, implications and recommendations you're delivering, then elevating the insight team in the organization and getting a seat at the table to aid in decision-making becomes much more achievable.

Having an insight community reduces your risk and builds your confidence in the decisions you make. You'll build customer engagement instead of breaking it down through ad hoc research projects. Your executives and others in the organization will call on you more often to help them make sense of Big Data whether that is transactional, behavioral, or social. Keeping a pulse on the ongoing voice of the customer is critical to stay ahead of the competition, and owning it should elevate your status in the organization.

Ellie Hutton is Vice President of Vision Critical University and a thought leader for Vision Critical, a software company specializing in connecting brands with their customers. For more information: www.visioncritical.com.

References
1. GreenBook. *Research Industry Trends Report.* Spring 2012. [Cited 2013 10 May]. Available from: http://www.greenbook.org/PDFs/GRIT-S12-Full.pdf
2. IBM. *What is big data?* 2013. [Cited 2013 10 May]; Article by IBM on Big Data]. Available from: http://www-01.ibm.com/software/data/bigdata/
3. Peter Harris. *Value of insight communities: Better business decisions.* March 7, 2013. [Cited 2013 10 May; Vision Critical Blog Post]. Available from: http://www.visioncritical.com/blog/value-insight-communities-better-business-decisions

SECTION FOUR
ANALYTICS

CHAPTER 10

Marketing Mix Modeling: Regression-Based or Agent-Based?

By Michael Shea and Sanjiv Gupta

Marketing Mix Modeling (MMM) has been in use since at least the 1990s, principally through the application of regression-based techniques. More recently around the early 2000's, agent-based computational modeling has also been applied to MMM. What follows is a brief discussion and framework on the relative strengths and weaknesses of both of these computationally valid methods.

Regression-Based Marketing Mix Modeling (RB MMM)
Most marketers and analysts know the basics behind RB MMM. Marketing mix modeling is an econometric approach that uses historic sales and causal data to quantify the impact of several marketing and promotional activities. Regression-based modeling is able to decompose sales of a product as driven by that product's distribution, price, and various marketing elements including temporary price reductions, types of media spend, as well as macro factors such as seasonality and consumer confidence. In doing so, it takes into account a wide range of sales and spending data both for a marketer's own brands and those of competitors. Various summaries and perspectives have been written about RB MMM [1, 2].

RB MMM is predominantly used to optimize sales volume or profit impact of various marketing and promotional levers as well as a sales forecasting tool. It's a very good, relative measure of short-term impact of all the brand drivers activities, thus allowing the marketer to make a fact-based decision on investment choices.

RB MMM was initially adopted by the CPG industry, with subsequent expansion into pharmaceuticals, retail and automotive, among others. Its adoption has been increasing over the years as syndicated data becomes readily available, as well as strategic implementation of results, which has delivered measurable improvement in the performance of brands and company's bottom line.

Agent-Based Marketing Mix Modeling (AB MMM)

The use of agent-based modeling is a relatively new approach to addressing MMM. While agent-based modeling (ABM) was conceptualized in the 1940's, advances in computational capabilities have allowed it to be increasingly applied in numerous fields including paleontology, anthropology, epidemiology, biological warfare, and economics. Most recently, it is also being applied to MMM, including commercial software solutions. Numerous articles have now been written to explain and advance the use of ABM [3]. Recent review articles about the use of ABM for the consumer market have also been published [4, 5, 6, 7].

The key feature of ABM is the computational use of "agents," which for MMM are typically representations of key types of consumers including their demographic and behavioral characteristics. It is important to note that while these agents are designed to be representative of individual consumers, they are neither numerous enough nor unique enough to be modeled (or thought of) as individuals per se. The inclusion of behavioral characteristics into the computational agents directly contributes to the key benefit of AB MMM, which is that it can join behavioral theory frameworks with empirical data. Once the behavioral characteristics of the agents have been validated by the empirical data, the AB model can be used to make predictions that are not just mere extensions of historical data.

A recent review of ABM for the consumer market [4] highlights the promise that it has for being a more holistic representation of the interdependencies of the decisions made by consumers, retailers, and manufacturers, particularly for repeated usage by the commercial sector and related professionals. Also, many in this field see that RBM and ABM can be used in a very complimentary fashion [4,5].

Let's look at the strengths and weaknesses of the two types of MMM:

Strengths of RB MMM

RB MMM has been around for nearly three decades. Thus it has been extensively proven and widely accepted across various industries. The methodology has been rigorously tested and applied. The results of this methodology are easily explained since the model directly correlates marketing levers to product sales, making it intuitive to understand.

This methodology has flexible capabilities in terms of geographic coverage, ranging from highly aggregated total U.S. to Hyper-Local to Store level. A lean version of RB MMM can be used to measure impact of marketing tests as well as conduct in-depth price elasticity analysis.

Weaknesses of RB MMM

Even though RB MMM provides extremely useful information for decision-making, there are a few weaknesses of this methodology which should also be taken into consideration. This methodology is dependent upon historic data to evaluate marketing performance. Therefore it is not a very effective way to measure new product performance given the lack of history and instability in the first few periods of launch. It is an excellent tool for measurement of short-term impact of sales drivers; however, it can under-estimate the longer-term impact of some marketing executions [7].

If the analysis is conducted on an aggregated basis, the bias can deliver results that might not be precise. This issue can be magnified in situations where the models are used for fragmented localized media affects. The recent fragmentation of media type and target poses some significant challenges to this methodology as well.

Strengths of AB MMM

AB MMM is reflective of "real world" consumer behavior conducted using simulated trained agents and their purchase behavior. This allows for the analysis of marketing tactics' effectiveness as a function of consumer groups. It becomes extremely useful if marketers and management want to target A/P spend to focus on particular consumer segments. Once the simulated agents are trained, remodeling becomes very easy, thus shortening the lead-time between data and insight as compared to regression based approach. Additionally, since the agent-based models are built from ground up, so they're not prone to aggregation bias.

Weaknesses of AB MMM

Acceptance of AB MMM has been slow by marketers as well as industry publications due to lack of commonly accepted standards of how to use ABM.

The results of ABM are driven by trained agents and their behavior in the simulated marketplace. If the agents are inadequately (or incorrectly) trained, they will not be reflective of real consumer behavior, and the output will be adversely affected.

Also, ABM is much more computationally complex then RBM, requiring more sophisticated computer programming and greater processing capabilities. This in turn means that the ABM methodology is not as readily accessible to modelers and requires specialized skills.

Adoption of Agent-Based Modeling

ABM is generally seen as introducing an intriguing new perspective on how to optimize marketing spends. However, it is understandably also being met with some resistance and questions regarding its underlying assumptions and value relative to the more traditional RBM. This hesitation includes the perception that ABM does not deal with real data, and that ABMs have so many parameters that they can fit any data [5]. However, these criticisms can be made of almost any type of modeling effort. They can be addressed by clearly showing how the ABM is reflective of the real-world situation it is modeling. This is readily accomplished through the appropriate use of the traditional modeling steps of verification and validation, to which any model should be subjected.

Contributing to the reluctance to adopt AB MMM is the point that AB modelers in the field of marketing research have paid little attention to validation issues [8], and in general by the lack of widely accepted standards for establishing rigorous ABM [5]. Consequently, there is a movement amongst market modelers to institute guidelines to help ensure rigor in ABM [e.g. 5, 9, 10, 11], particularly because of the recognition that ABM has significant advantages and additional insights around MMM.

	Regression-Based MMM	Agent-Based MMM	
Pros	• Traditionally done using econometric models (regression-based) • Easily explained since model directly correlates marketing levels to product sales • Marketing tactics effectiveness by geography. Can tune the mix by geography. Can theoretical model individual store.	• Done using simulated trained agents (50K+) and their purchase behavior • Marketing tactics effectiveness work by consumer group. Can tune the mix to reach targeted segments. • Remodeling is easier once the agents are trained • More stable over the longer term	Pros
Cons	• Updates/remodeling are time intensive • Highly aggregated • Difficulty pulling apart simultaneous effects • Difficult integrating digital media measurements. Marketplace has become highly fragmented, can't effectively measure new touch points due to insufficient historical spend/sales data.	• Normally, challenging to explain since models are consumer attribute based • Non-representative at the individual consumer/disaggregated level • Garbage in Garbage Out – Model outcome is highly dependent on how well the agents have been trained	Cons

Table 1 – Key Strengths and Weaknesses of Regression-Based and Agent-Based MMM

Conclusion and Key Takeaways

Properly carried out, both RB and AB MMM approaches are perfectly valid and analytically rigorous. However, the two types of MMM have strengths and weakness relative to one another, as we have highlighted in this chapter. Knowledge of these attributes will allow marketing professionals to use the best approach to address their specific issues at hand.

Select the type of MMM that best addresses your marketing issues. In general, RB MMM is best at tackling the influence of marketing mix elements directly upon sales, while AB MMM is best at examining individual-based consumer behavior relative to the influence of the marketing mix elements. Relatedly, RB MMM is particularly good at measuring sales ROI, while AB MMM is particularly good at measuring Brand Equity ROI.

In the spirit of helping ensure that all MMM models are computationally robust and sufficiently reflective of reality, we encourage end-users to be as appropriately involved throughout the modeling process as their interests and capabilities dictate. While there will be analytical and proprietary limits, these should be able to be defined and explained. We further believe that the results of the modeling will be both improved and implementable through a healthy collaboration between the modelers and the end users.

Dr. Michael Shea is an Executive Vice President, and Sanjiv Gupta is a Director of Advanced Analytics at AMG Strategic Advisors, a division of Acosta Sales and Marketing. For more information: www.acosta.com.

References

1. J. Eliashberg and G. Lilien, 1993. "Mathematical Marketing Models: Some Historical Perspectives and Future Projections." Chapter 1 in *Handbooks in OR & MS*, 5:3-23.

2. G. Tellis, 2006. "Chapter 24-Marketing Mix Modeling" in *The Handbook of Marketing Research*, by Grover and Vriens, SAGE Publications.

3. C. Macal and M. North, 2010. "Tutorial on agent-based modelling and simulation." *Journal of Simulation*, 4:151-162

4. North et al, 2009. "Multiscale agent-based consumer market modeling." Complexity, 15:37-47

5. W. Rand and R.T. Rust, 2011."Agent-based modeling in marketing: Guidelines for rigor." *International Journal of Research in Marketing*, 28: 181-193

6. Gilbert et al, 2007. "Complexities in markets: Introduction to the special issue." *Journal of Business Research*, 60(8): 813-815.

7. S.A. Delre et al, 2007. "Targeting and timing of promotional activities: An agent-based model for the takeoff of new products." *Journal of Business Research*, 60(8): 826-835.

8. M. Ataman et at, 2010. "The long-term effect of marketing strategy on brand sales."*Journal of Marketing Research*, 47:866-882

9. R. Garcia, P. Rummel, and J. Hauser, 2007. "Validating agent-based marketing models through conjoint analysis." *Journal of Business Research*, 60(8): 848-857.

10. P. Windrum, G. Fagiolo, A. Moneta, 2007. "Empirical Validation of Agent-Based Models: Alternatives and Prospects", *Journal of Artificial Societies and Social Simulation, 10/2*, 8

11. G. Fagiolo, A. Moneta, P. Windrum, 2007. "A critical guide to empirical validation of agent-based models in economics: methodologies, procedures and open problems." *Computational Economics*, 30:195-226.

CHAPTER 11

Understanding Big Data

By Janet Dorenkott

Big Data is all the buzz today, but why? Hasn't Big Data been around for years? The answer is yes, but no. The Big Data they refer to today is different. Big Data is not just about data volume, it's about the structure and how we handle Big Data that is evolving.

The term Big Data can be confusing because most companies have huge data volumes. And what we use to handle Big Data volumes can involve a variety of technologies including relational databases, MPP platforms, distributed cloud environments, cubes, in memory databases, etc.

However, today there is a new technology called Hadoop, which uses Map Reduce to handle Big Data. There are also other technologies such as Teradata's Aster that handle unstructured data in other ways that are also very efficient.

When companies talk about Big Data today, they are referring to data that is not structured. Examples of unstructured data include social chatter, media files, geo-mapping, digital files, diagrams, schematics, blueprints, videos, click stream, speech to text, etc. Structured data, on the other hand, would be data found in order entry systems, manufacturing systems, accounting applications, etc. Data that comes from

SAP, JDE and other internal applications have structured data. To put it simply, data that is not easily broken down is unstructured.

Think about social media data, for example. By social media, I am referring to chatter, discussions, blogs, etc. I am not referring to clickstream analysis (although that is another form of Big Data). Say a customer complains about Product A on Twitter. The company who owns Product A will want to respond to that individual and try to make them happy, or otherwise neutralize that person's comment. If the company is successful at making the author happy, they have changed their sentiment. However, a company may have a series of negative comments from many users. The company must respond quickly to change that sentiment.

By breaking down that chatter into positive, negative and neutral sentiment, companies can compare sentiment day to day and see if their neutralization efforts were successful or not. But to do this, they need to break that chatter down into a structured format. They then need to pull it into a database that can analyze that data against internal data. This is where Big Data meets the DSR (Demand Signal Repository) and the data warehouse to improve business intelligence.

Big Data is important to business users because it can be used to improve business, increase sales, cut costs, streamline efficiencies, and improve sentiment.

Big Data is often associated with data warehousing and business intelligence. But data warehousing and business intelligence have been around for years. Big Data, as it pertains to structured data, has been integrated into data warehouse and business intelligence applications. However, as new data sources evolve, integrating and using that more complex data so that it provides value has become a new hurdle for companies. It has made the requirement for a sound infrastructure more important than ever before.

Back in the '80s, a hundred gig was considered Big Data in terms of volume. Terabytes were something most companies didn't concern themselves with. But in 1992, Teradata built the first system with over 1 TB for Wal-Mart. That was considered Big Data. Petabytes were not even considered reality.

Teradata has their massively parallel processing databases (MPP) to handle Massive Data. Massive Data sounds a lot bigger than Big Data.

I believe it was Oracle that coined the acronym VLDB for Very Large Database. Oracle actively created marketing campaigns leveraging VLDB terminology, which originally represented databases over a terabyte that offered partitioning options. Again, Very Large Database sounds bigger to me than Big Data. But as technology evolves, we need to identify new ways to handle it.

What was considered Big Data in the '90s is not necessarily what the technology marketing folks are referring to as Big Data today. This time around, Big Data is even bigger and it's different! Some people think of Big Data as anything outside of their ERP systems or data warehouse. That's not actually correct. That's because data outside your firewall that you want to bring in often does have some structure to it. It may not be consistent, but it has structure. Therefore, it does not fit the pure Big Data definition that exists today. However, I do understand this thinking because if you want data to have value – structured or unstructured – you have to format it in a way that will allow you to integrate it in a manageable way with internal data. So how do we do this?

If we consider Big Data as unstructured data, then we have to add structure to make it usable. In this way, Big Data becomes structured and part of the overall, enterprise infrastructure . The enterprise data sources can be vast and can include data from internal systems as well as outside data.

Integrating data for any industry is complicated, but for the consumer goods industry, the complexities are compounded. Consumer goods manufacturers not only have the standard data integration issues that come along with integrating data from internal data sources, but they have the added complexity of integrating all the sources outside their business sent to them by retailers, syndicated data providers, distributors and other outside data they may purchase. Now add to that social media chatter.

Years ago, retailers would never dream of sharing their point-of-sale (POS) data. Today, most of them share it in some way, shape or form. In fact, that's one of the issues. They all share differently. File types are different. They may use a data provider. They may offer a portal. They may offer POS in EDI files. They may send flat files. There are many ways each individual retailer could offer access to POS data. Even EDI files, which have a standardized format, are not "standardized" as they should be.

In addition, the formats retailers send the data in are different. Data elements vary from company to company. Some retailers may offer inventory information, others do not. The granularity of data received is different. Some will give store and item level detail. Some will only offer weekly or brand level detail. It varies from retailer to retailer.

Continuity and timing are also issues with POS data. Some send minimal data on a weekly or monthly basis; others offer daily-level detail, down to the store on a daily basis; some retailers don't send data at all. Even data that is supposed to be sent on a scheduled basis might be off by a few days. Often those feeds include duplicates or are missing days of data.

Many retailers offer data through syndicated data providers like Nielsen, IRI and NPD. Third-party data providers often have delays associated with their data. Multiple hierarchies and calendars are an issue with POS data as well. All of this lends to the growing volume and variety of data.

So you get the fact that integrating POS data is complex, but wait. It's getting more complex. Enriching the data by applying metrics and formulas to that data also adds complexity and volume.

Now let's consider other forms of potential Big Data. How about emerging markets? What is emerging market data and why is there a dilemma associated with it? Emerging market data is data coming from countries like Taiwan, Hong Kong, India, Nigeria, Chile, etc.

What makes emerging market data so much different from the POS data you get in the states or Europe? A lot! Frequency, new data formats, new data types, sophistication of the sender, retailer size, products sold, consumers, quantities, etc. Just about every aspect of the sales process is different in emerging markets.

Compare a U.S.-based retailer with an emerging market retailer. Wal-Mart offers a wide variety of data. A CPG manufacturer can access Wal-Mart data and access reports based on their job function. They can download reports and that data can be integrated into an enterprise demand signal repository. Compare that with an emerging market retailer. Unlike the U.S. and Europe, emerging market retailers tend to be individuals who own individual stores. They rarely even own more than one. Wal-Mart on the other hand, owns thousands of stores, as does Target, Tesco, Ahold, etc. So the make-up of the retailer is very different. In addition, the stores tend to be small and carry scarce variety, small quantities and limited inventory.

Now let's compare the POS data itself. Most emerging market retailers don't have cash registers. They are not uploading sales information to corporate on a nightly basis. Their way of tracking inventory is the owner manually counting the items on the shelf in most cases. Their POS is not really POS. In most cases, it's order information. Now consider the order information. It's also not typically being ordered through any sophisticated system. Usually, the proprietor is using an application on their cell phone to place an order back to a distributor. The distributor is often then transmitting or forwarding that order back to the manufacturer. Therefore, in most cases, POS data from emerging markets is not POS data at all. It's order data or sometimes shipment data. Aligning that data correctly and validating that data is a very complex process.

Next, consider data types. Although many retail owners in the emerging market are very savvy with their cell phone applications, the applications aren't always the same. On top of that, they may be submitting information via an app, email, or simply in a flat file. Data cleanliness issues with emerging market retailers are not only more complex, they are much more unknown and untested. And let's not forget the complications related to currency conversions and volatility of currency. Currency conversion actually becomes a new data source as well, depending on how a company wants to handle them. This can be unstructured, depending on the source and can be considered Big Data.

Social media chatter also represents massive data volumes. Depending on your company, what you want to collect, and how you plan to use social media data, the data volumes can be mind boggling. Some companies run ads on social media and just want to collect click stream information for analysis. Others want to gather chatter – good, bad or indifferent – that people are posting about their company and align that with sales to provide immediate response.

Loyalty data and market basket are also adding to Big Data. Think about every person who scans a loyalty card. The information you wrote out on that card includes personal information. It also can include profile information that includes everything from your age to what you buy and what you bought with your shampoo, for example. Market basket adds to the Big Data concept.

Big Data is being defined by some software companies today as unstructured. But when you integrate unstructured data with structured data, you could still be talking massive data volumes. The trick is taking just the data elements you need from the unstructured data to integrate with structured data. Putting some form of structure behind it that will allow you to gain a better understanding of your customer and improve business is the main value to Big Data. Having a sound infrastructure that will allow for the integration of various data sources has become a necessity.

Janet Dorenkott is co-founder and COO of Relational Solutions, Inc. The North Olmsted, Ohio-based software and service company specializes in demand signal repositories, data integration, data warehousing and business intelligence for consumer goods companies. For more information: www.relationalsolutions.com.

CHAPTER 12

The Incredible Dissolving Store Revisited

By James Tenser

Online shopping 1.0 was bringing the store to the Web. Now with mobile technology we're in shopping 2.0 — how do you bring the Web to the store?

VenkyHarinarayan, Co-founder, Kosmix, SVP Walmart Global e-Commerce and Head of @WalmartLabs, in *Scientific American* blog, Nov. 11, 2011

It used to be pretty easy to separate in-store marketing from the rest of the consumer marketing agenda. During the early 1990s, the boundaries were firm and fixed; the channels at retail were few and fairly straight-forward: instant coupons, signs, deals, displays, various types of static media.

Media advertising and consumer promotion were distinct sectors with distinct budgets that flowed *outside* the store in familiar channels such as television, direct mail and newspaper circulars. Their role was to create awareness, build demand, and stimulate trips. We would close the deal at the shelf later, using the in-store vehicles.

Two decades have elapsed and now the in-store versus out-of-store distinction seems quaint and obsolete. Frequent shopper card programs, online sites and mobile apps have enabled retailers to extend in-store interaction out toward shoppers in their homes and lives, creating new options for behaviorally targeted persuasion. Incredibly powerful mobile devices have enabled shoppers to invite the rest of the world in on command, while they are in the act of shopping our stores – to access product information, competitive pricing, and the opinions and counsel of peers.

The Walls Have Pores

Technology and social trends cause the boundaries between in-store and in-life to become more permeable every day. You might say the walls of the store are becoming more and more *porous*, with profound implications for retailers, brands and shoppers.

Social, search, and location-based interactions, enabled by online and mobile technology, are forever changing how we may understand "presence" in the physical domain. The aisles have become "endless" as assortments are extended into the virtual world. Brick-and-mortar stores are at times reduced to showrooms for the rest of the e-tail universe. Reviews, promotional deals and competing prices flow into shoppers' hands with a stunning absence of friction.

> *Brands that actually engage shoppers, experientially or emotionally, tend to turn shoppers into buyers. ... If brands can engage shoppers near or at the point of decision, more often than not, they can close the sale.*
>
> Rafe Ring (2011), *Turning Shoppers into Buyers*, OgilvyAction, the Ogilvy Group's brand activation company

More Info, Less Control

All these personal data-generating activities – social, mobile, local and search transactions and media consumption – leave behind a data footprint that is vast and varied. Many observers describe this generally as "Big Data," or sometimes SoMoLoMe. Big Data possesses several traits that are remarkable and unprecedented:

1. ***It's BIG.*** Not just regular big, but big on a scale never before encountered. It's so big that our regular analytic tools are pretty near useless for comprehending it. That means new strategies and technologies are needed. A lot of people are working on that.

2. ***It grows incredibly fast.*** More people are using online, social, mobile and connected technologies for more purposes every day, and the bandwidth of their individual contributions to the total flow keeps expanding at an expanding rate.

3. ***It's both structured and un-structured.*** That's because it's an amalgam of text, image, audio, video and tabular data. This accounts in large measure for its rapid expansion, since media files contain a lot of data.

4. ***It's in the cloud.*** Big Data isn't on your server. It wouldn't fit. It's actually spread across server farms in bunkers and office buildings and hollow mountains all over the place.

5. ***It generates metadata about itself.*** Big Data, especially the SoMoLoMe elements, are about both message content and messaging action. That means even if we ignore what a post, message, transaction or transmitted file actually says, its existence constitutes a data point, as do the sender, recipient, time, date, place, size, etc. This data, in aggregate, is an enormous source of behavioral insights.

The grand scale of this new data – affecting both consumer behavior and business practices – seems to threaten the integrity of the box itself. In The Incredible Dissolving Store, we have *boundary issues*.

Critical business information about shoppers now flows both within and without the physical store. Behavioral influences are no longer confined to the area at or near the shelf. The messages we painstakingly plan and craft using conventional media and promotions are intersecting with new, powerful influences that are *out of our control*. This threatens to undermine the stable processes that have served us somewhat faithfully for the past two decades. Still, many retailers hold fast to their world views; for example, according to a study released by Edgell Knowledge Network, 80 percent of retailers are aware of Big Data, but only 47 percent are clear about its implications for their business.

While social and mobile channels provide avenues for retailers to be cutting-edge, the consensus among the [retail] executives we surveyed is that brick-and-mortar stores are still the leading format for providing higher service levels and building brand awareness.

Deloitte's Store 3.0 Survey: The Next Evolution, September 2011

Brick-and-mortar is still alive and well. Mobile is actually going to increase the consumer experience while they're shopping, so retailers need to embrace it.

David Dorf, Oracle Retail, in Retail TouchPoints (2011) The Store: The Intersection Of All Channels, eBook sponsored by Oracle

The New Big

So how big are we talking? Well the numbers are changing fast, but the user statistics are impressive. Here are some eye-opening worldwide stats[1]:

- **2.4 billion** – Number of internet users worldwide

- **6.7 billion** – Number of mobile phone subscriptions worldwide

- **3.3 billion** – Number of Google searches per day

- **2.7 billion** – Number of Facebook likes per day

- **175 million** – Number of Twitter interactions per day

- **28.8 million** – Number of Walmart customer transactions per day[2]

All this user activity over the Web, mobile and social media adds up to some pretty breathtaking quantities of data. Remember when a retailer installing a terabyte-sized database was considered a newsworthy investment? Now it's not unusual for a household to have a network drive that can hold one or two terabytes or more of media files and backups for less than $200.

The total amount of digital information in the world in 2012 reached 2.7 zettabytes, an increase of 48 percent over 2011, according to an IDC report[3] How big is a zettabyte? That's 10^{21} bytes, or 1,000,000,000,000,000,000,000 or a billion terabytes or one with 21 zeroes after it. By comparison a terabyte is only 10^{12} bytes.

This mind-boggling volume is increasingly captured in unstructured form, driven by such data-hungry inputs as SoMoLoMe activity, video and sensor data captured in public places, including the shopper-detecting systems now proliferating in retail stores. Plenty more is generated due to evolving shopper behaviors:

- Multichannel shopping is the new norm (*>50% of customers make multichannel purchases that combine search, research, online and store in varying combinations*)

- Social media keeps exploding (*>78% of customers trust peer recommendations about brands and products*)

- Mobile commerce comes on strong (*>38% of smartphone owners have made a purchase using their devices*)

- Online shopping keeps chugging (*>15% growth year over year*).

Big Data visionaries postulate that brands and retailers will soon be routinely mining these external and internal data flows for relevant behavioral insights and applying those insights to assortment, replenishment, price, promotional and markdown decisions. The challenge is that the old familiar methods for digging out shopper insights might not work so well in the new era.

Big Data is so big and so fast-growing that it *cannot reside in a single system*. Got a favorite spreadsheet or analytics package? You may never get past the data download if you try to use it to tap Big Data. If, for example, you try to incorporate it into the first step of the 8-step Category Management process – Category Assessment – Big Data would ensure you would never finish step one.

Solutions are on their way. Apache Hadoop is an open-source software framework that supports data-intensive distributed computing. Its proponents assert that 80 percent of the world's data is "unstructured" and that its value is therefore inaccessible. A lot of very smart people are collaborating on Hadoop development to unlock its power. Eventually, it will enable us to extract the useful bits out of Big Data flows. An example might be tracking local Facebook sentiment to help plan variations in store assortments.

> *Our go-to-market strategy is to win wherever people shop. ... As more people move their shopping habits online, we want to be present when and where they want to make a purchase.*
>
> Alex Tosolini, Vice President of Global e-Business, Procter & Gamble, 2012

> *A compelling brand value message [is needed] that provides a persuasive reason, other than a coupon, for a website visitor to buy the brand.*
>
> Accenture, comScore, dunnhumbyUSA, *Are Your CPG Brands Maximizing the Return on Your Digital Investment?* 2012

Thought Experiment

So what are we to make of Shopper Marketing and Category Management in a world where these forces swirl? More importantly, what practical in-store actions can we anticipate folding into today's routine processes once we learn to tap the outside insights of Big Data?

I challenge readers with the following thought experiment: Try to visualize what life could be like for retail and brand professionals in a world with vastly *more information* and a good deal *less control*.

We may identify ten or more sources of input that a Category Manager of the future might incorporate into planning decisions. Many are already familiar: Optimization of assortment, price, promotion and markdowns are well-established techniques built into software suites for retailers. Some vendors offer macro space-planning solutions, automated replenishment, capacity planning, in-store implementation and competitive analytics solutions.

Shopper success — and therefore, the success of our category and promotional plans — is influenced by all these factors. Simultaneously. Continuously.

All these new data-based influences mean the locus of power is rapidly leaving the store and distributing across your customers' mobile devices. Imagine routinely mining these external data flows for relevant behavioral insights and applying those insights on a continuous basis to enable shopper success and sustain meaningful competitive advantage.

Now picture the boundaries of the in-store environment vanishing – what I call The Incredible Dissolving Store.

> *An increasingly complex, non-linear buying process requires a different, cross-channel approach—one that puts brands wherever*

consumers are, in a way that encourages participation, not passive consumption of marketing messages.

Economist Intelligence Unit, *New Directions Consumer Goods Companies Hone a Cross-channel Approach to Consumer Marketing,* Sponsored by Oracle 2012

There is a massive intersection of things happening in social media and in the stores. A lot of information is extending downstream from marketing channels into the store. We need to present useful information that they can act on at the point of purchase.

Venky Balakrishnan, Vice President of Marketing Innovation, Diageo 2012

Leap-Frogging Loyalty Cards

When SoMoLoMe comes into the picture, suddenly even data-intensive frequent shopper card programs seem, with the benefit of hindsight, to be not terribly exotic. There may be other ways to segment shoppers that don't require sign-ups or the incentives of constant deals.

It may be argued that we are entering into a *post-loyalty era* in which extracts of Big Data might be a preferable alternative to card data. If this comes to pass, then the stout refusal of some very big retailers to establish frequent shopper programs may look like acts of genius.

A recent innovation by Wal-Mart is looking like just such a bid to leap-frog the loyalty card. The chain already established an individual Facebook page for each of its U.S. retail locations more than a year ago. Presumably it can monitor sentiment on those pages, and apply any learnings to local merchandising tactics.

More recently it began introducing a mobile shopper app called Scan & Go, developed by its @Walmartlabs unit in Silicon Valley. Already available for 214 stores, it was described by one columnist recently as "the back door to a CRM system..."

The @Walmartlabs folks aren't shy about this either. Here's a description from their web site:

> *We believe the mobile phone can bring amazing experiences into our customers' hands. But the future isn't just on the phone; it's in the combination of mobile technology and our 10,000+ stores. Over 200 million customers visit our stores worldwide each week, and we plan to give each one of them a reason to use their phones to enhance their in-store experience. From mobile payments to richer product information to local store information, the mobile apps and sites we build will bring real-time information and helpful tools to make shopping experiences easier and more enjoyable.*
>
> http://www.walmartlabs.com/mobile/

Wal-Mart can perceive the walls dissolving. It has stated in the recent past that its U.S. shopper base is so large that it is an effective proxy for the entire population. That works both ways. Who needs loyalty cards when it can mine social media and mobile app interactions for all the insights it needs? You don't need to buy card membership with deals to make that happen.

Ongoing Discomfort

It becomes increasingly apparent that retail and brand marketing in the Incredible Dissolving Store will not be about *solving the equation* — it will be about *tuning the system*. New analytics tools make the keys to relevance more accessible and more automated than ever. The lifecycles of decisions are consequently shorter than ever.

Shopper marketing, once focused on influencing shoppers at a few moments of truth, is rapidly widening to encompass multiple brand and retail interactions that take place at home, online, in social media, in public, and in the store in a constantly varying sequence. Methods for targeting and monitoring performance in this matrix are coming on fast, but there is little uniformity.

Category Management, like it or not, is rapidly shifting from an orderly, controlled, recursive, planning process with boundaries and well-defined metrics into a deliberately dis-orderly, multidimensional, broad, shape-shifting and organic process that incorporates planning, detection, response and continuous strategic reconsideration.

Frequent shopper programs – and the one-to-one marketing ideal – are now under reconsideration by some in the context of SoMoLoMe. Other ways are emerging to segment and target that don't require deep deals as the incentive to participate. Cards aren't going away just yet, but apps are poised to usurp them.

The walls of the store mean less and less. Merchandising decisions will be more localized. Performance more visible. Participants more accountable. Corrections more possible and more rapid.

In the Incredible Dissolving Store, we need to get used to the kind of ongoing discomfort that these changes will bring and think very carefully about the metrics we will use to define success. If we listen actively and shed our bias, the shoppers will tell us what those must be.

James Tenser is Principal, VSN Strategies, a content marketing advisory firm that prides itself on exceptional vision, value generation and thought leadership. For more information: http://vsnstrategies.com

References
1. http://royal.pingdom.com/2013/01/16/internet-2012-in-numbers/
2. Walmart.com corporate web site 2012 "200 million per week" across all channels.
3. http://www.forbes.com/sites/ciocentral/2012/05/01/big-data-the-hidden-opportunity/

CHAPTER 13

Evolving from Product Warehouses to Retail Experiences

By Eric Seiberling

Many retailers have a new four-letter word in their vocabulary. It is called "showrooming." That is when shoppers scope out products at a local retailer, compare prices online using mobile devices in the store, and then buy them from the cheapest source. In some ways, it is like a legal form of shoplifting. The retail store does all of the work, yet online retailers get the benefits.[28]

Many retailers have expressed deep concern that this trend will continue to grow as more customers leave the store without a trip to the cash register. But a Columbia Business School and AIMIA report, *Showrooming and the Rise of the Mobile-Assisted Shopper,* shows that "only 6% of mobile shoppers already plan to buy online when they walk into a store, while 30% are committed to purchase in the store, but using mobile to look for additional information to guide their decision."[29] Retailers are using additional price incentives, free

---

28 Stock, Kyle. "Maybe Showrooming Isn't Killing Retailers After All." BloomberyBusinessweek. September 12, 2013. http://www.businessweek.com/articles/2013-09-12/maybe-showrooming-isnt-killing-retailers-after-all
29 Quint, Matthew, David Rodgers and Rick Ferguson."Showrooming and the Rise of the Mobile Assisted Shopper."Columbia Business School and AIMIA. September 2013. http://www8.gsb.columbia.edu/globalbrands/m-shopper-research

delivery, and loyalty programs to prevent the customer from walking out their doors and purchasing the product somewhere else.

What we need to realize is that this is not a new phenomenon. Local mom and pop stores experienced showrooming when shoppers used their experienced staff to understand different products and then left to buy them at the Walmart down the block. Grocery stores saw customers stop buying basic food and household items as they purchased many of their essential needs at a lower price in bulk at the local club store. Online stores have challenged brick-and-mortar retailers in the same way.

Showrooming is not the death knell of retail. It is nothing more than an attempt to make sense of a shifting retail landscape as new options are made available. Consumers are now empowered with more information, product choices, and buying venues than ever. In other words, the market has become much "flatter" and retailers need to rethink how they will compete for shopper's attention and dollars as they reevaluate their purchase behaviors based on price, convenience, previous experiences, service, and other factors.

Evolving from a Product Warehouse to a Retail Experience

We are seeing an accelerating evolution of the shopping experience. Since the first grocery store was launched by Piggly Wiggly in 1916, the concept of the retail environment as a self-service product warehouse was born. Different packaged goods are warehoused together to be able to meet the demands for a consumer. As grocery expanded into mass, club, c-store and dollar formats, the form factor remained relatively the same.

Online retailers have changed the playing field by combining a wide variety of products and low prices with the convenience of both easy shopping and home delivery. Now consumers can shop a broader set of "warehouses" for the best deal and even get free delivery. This is increasing the pressure to compete on price, and pushing retailers to leverage trade promotion management and price optimization to create the best "offer" to shoppers.

As all of these different channels compete on price, profit margins are gettting squeezed. Chains like Best Buy, Sears, JC Penney and many other consumer goods and electronic stores have closed thousands of stores, while a number of marquee retail chains like Circuit City and Borders have ceased to exist. Wal-Mart's "Everyday low price" and the recession since 2008 have placed a number of retailers in distress and struggling to stay afloat.

As an additional threat, there is a re-emergence of online grocery shopping and home delivery. Companies have learned from the failures of Webvan, and others and are slowly developing viable home delivery models. Amazon.com plans to expand its AmazonFresh's online grocery business to up to 40 urban markets after five years of testing in its hometown of Seattle.[30] Likewise, Wal-Mart has been testing its overnight and same-day delivery of online grocery orders in San Francisco, while companies like Fresh Direct and Safeway are making headway to deliver fresh produce, milk, meat and other products ordered online.[31] These providers appear to be building the infrastructure necessary to cherry pick high-end grocery shoppers from the market similar to what has happened in the electronics, music, and book industries.

A July 2013 survey by Market Force Information may offer some insight into how retailers can break the "commoditization of retail." Their survey was designed to discover where consumers prefer to shop and why they favor one grocery chain over another. It also analyzed where they spent the majority of their money over the past 30 days to understand actual purchase behavior.[32]

According to the survey, Trader Joe's, Publix, Whole Foods, Wegmans,

---

30 "Amazon Plans Major Move Into Grocery Business." Reuters. June 4, 2013. http://www.cnbc.com/id/100789495
31 Wells, Jane. "Your next meal may come compliments of Amazon." CNBC, July 26, 2013. http://www.cnbc.com/id/100916844
32 "Trader Joe's is Consumers Favorite Grocery Chain, According to Market Force Study." Marketforce. July 24, 2014 http://www.marketforce.com/press-releases/item/trader-joes-is-consumers-favorite-grocery-chain-according-to-market-force-study-/

and ALDI ranked high on the consumer delight index. These retailers have found the right mix of selection, pricing and promotions and designed shopper experiences for their high-value consumers. As a result, these chains are experiencing high single-digit growth and stronger margins while the grocery industry revenues have declined 1.3% over the same period. These growing retailers have created unique experiences that spark with their shoppers.

Discount retailers like Wal-Mart rated lower both in terms of satisfaction and recommendation by consumers, suggesting that price – while important – does not drive where people shop. According to the report, top performers "received high marks for courteous staff, inviting atmosphere and high quality produce." This represents a subtle shift where price may not be "king." The importance of operational issues, an integrated shopping experience, and created social experiences inside the store can change the game and reduce the commoditization of retail.

Retailers must differentiate themselves in the marketplace both against brick-and-mortar stores and online competitors. This requires a change from a warehouse mentality for products to creating shopping experiences for their consumers. Retailers need to have a deep understanding of the target shopper and their needs, and then design the right mix of pricing, products and experience to meet them.

Defining Retail Experiences

Joseph Pine and James Gilmore were among the first to identify this shift from products to experiences in their 1999 book, "The Experience Economy: Work Is Theatre & Every Business a Stage," in which they warned that big-name stores could be in trouble. They studied the evolution of business and articulated "The Progression of Economic Value" from commodities to goods to services to experiences.[33] At each stage, the price for the buyer and the margin for the seller increased by an order of magnitude. Two cents worth of coffee beans

---

33   Pine, Joseph B. and James H. Gilmore. "Welcome to the Experience Economy." Harvard Business Review, July 1998. http://hbr.org/1998/07/welcome-to-the-experience-economy/

(commodity) can be sold for 10 cents as ground coffee in the grocery store (product), one dollar at McDonald's or Dunkin Donuts (service), and for $3 to $5 at Starbucks (experience). As competition and expectations rise, products and services are becoming commoditized in the minds of consumers.

This same progression has also happened in retail. Cooking classes at Sur La Table, rock-climbing walls at REI, and golf-swing simulators at Dick's Sporting Goods are all efforts to create experiences in store that drive traffic and sales in store – and some are even charging for the experience.[34] They offer experiences that cannot be found anywhere else to attract shoppers and drive loyalty.

A look at the leaders of a Market Force survey shows that they all have created elements of a distinctive shopper experience. Each one takes a unique approach to transform itself from a product warehouse into a shopping experience that delights consumers and meets their needs. For example:

- **Trader Joe's** creates an "an offbeat, fun discovery zone that elevates food shopping from a chore to a cultural experience."[35]

- **Publix** is beating Wal-Mart in the grocery game by focusing on service and quality over price, yet delivering 5.6% net margins in 2012 vs. Wal-Mart's 3.8%.[36]

- **Whole Foods** focuses on healthy eating and sustainability to create "America's Healthiest Grocery Store" and guides every

---

34 O'Connell, Jonathan. "In the experience economy, retailers are selling much more than goods." Washington Post, December 7, 2013. http://articles.washingtonpost.com/2012-12-07/opinions/35673581_1_geek-squad-big-name-stores-retailers

35 Kowitt, Beth. "Inside the secret world of Trader Joe's." Money.com. August 23, 2010. http://money.cnn.com/2010/08/20/news/companies/inside_trader_joes_full_version.fortune/index.htm

36 Solomon, Brian. "The Wal-Mart Slayer: How Publix's People-First Culture Is Winning The Grocer War" Forbes, July 24, 2013. http://www.forbes.com/sites/briansolomon/2013/07/24/the-wal-mart-slayer-how-publixs-people-first-culture-is-winning-the-grocer-war/

element of their store design, product selection and marketing to deliver on this promise.[37]

- **Wegmans'** personal touch and "European open-air" feel has enabled it to take nearly every top retail honor available, including an award from *Child* magazine for being "the most family-friendly supermarket in America."[38]

- **ALDI's** tight focus on cost conscious shoppers offers great products at the lowest possible prices in a simple and easy-to-navigate shopping environment.[39]

While it takes greater time, effort and cost to create these shopper experiences, it has paid off with rich financial dividends and greater shopper loyalty even during a recession. Each of them has keenly understood the desired shopper experience, how they shop, and orchestrated their time in store to deliver against their expectations. ALDI's "warehouse" feel would not appeal to the Trader Joe's shopper – and they do not have to. Instead, they deeply understand what their specific shopper wants and deliver it every time.

Shoppers Want Experiences, Not Transactions

Shopping can be a chore. On some level, stores can be viewed as nothing more than transactional environments – just places to put products on shelves. Many store environments create confusion and make it difficult for shoppers to find what they want to buy, whether they are modern trade or high frequency store layouts. As with any chore, shoppers want to get their shopping done as fast as possible, at the lowest cost to themselves.

But what if shopping can become something that is delightful and

---

37 Whole Foods Corporate Website.http://www.wholefoodsmarket.com/company-info
38 Abelson, Jenn. "First taste of Wegmans experience." Boston.com. October 9, 2011. http://www.boston.com/business/articles/2011/10/09/first_taste_of_the_wegmans_experience/?page=full
39 Simms, Natalie. "Publix, ALDI to offer very different grocery shopping experiences." Hometown headlines, July 29, 2013. http://johndruckenmiller.com/publix-aldi-to-offer-very-different-grocery-shopping-experiences/

where they want to spend their time and money? Wharton's Jay H. Baker Retailing Initiative teamed with Verde and the Retail Council of Canada to discover how retailers can create an extraordinary experience for shoppers.[40] The report titled *Discovering 'WOW' – A Study of Great Retail Shopping Experiences in North America*, points to five major areas that contribute to a great shopping experience:

- *Engagement*: Being polite, genuinely caring and interested in helping, acknowledging and listening.

- *Executional Excellence*: Patiently explaining and advising, checking stock, helping to find products, having product knowledge and providing unexpected product quality.

- *Brand Experience*: Exciting store design and atmosphere, consistently great product quality, making customers feel they're special and that they always get a deal.

- *Expediting:* Being sensitive to customers' time on long checkout lines, being proactive in helping speed the shopping process.

- *Problem Recovery*: Helping resolve and compensate for problems, upgrading quality and ensuring complete satisfaction.

If we take a step back and review these elements, many of these issues can be addressed in the design of the store before a problem occurs. Simplifying the shopping experience by getting the basic assortment and merchandising right, improving the store layout and navigation to fit the way the consumer shops, and designing the right atmosphere and branding to create an emotional bond with the shopper will set the stage for a delightful experience. This will help store personnel to engage the shopper, avoid execution issues and problems and help expedite their shopping trip.

---

40 "Getting to 'Wow': Consumers Describe What Makes a Great Shopping Experience" Knowledge@Wharton, July 8, 2009. http://knowledge.wharton.upenn.edu/article.cfm?articleid=2275

Defining the Consumer Journey Using Virtual Reality

It starts with the shopper journey. McKinsey & Company consultant Dorian Stone and John Devine, in their report *From Moments to Journeys: A Paradigm Shift in Customer Experience Excellence*, ask a question: Why are customer loyalty and engagement so slow to improve while the business reports positive customer feedback after every interaction? Their analysis found that focusing on "moments of truth" provides too fragmented of a view of the customer. Customer loyalty and perception is based on the sum of interactions around a specific need, which they call a Consumer Journey.[41]

Both CPG manufacturers and retailers need to view the sum total of the entire shopping experience, while today's tools focus on a specific category or department of a store. Transaction logs (t-logs) show a shopper's basket size and items, but miss the emotional components involved in the shopping experience. Category management, price optimization and trade promotion tools are focused on the choices and prices a shopper makes, but fail to understand the motivations behind the choices.

In the past, it was quite expensive to conduct consumer research in the context of the shelf and store. Retailers would either need to disrupt current store operations to conduct research or need to mock up shopping environments in specialized research facilities. Only the largest CPG companies could create their own "research stores" in innovation centers, spending hundreds of thousands of dollars to test a single store format and constantly purchasing competitive products to create a realistic store.

It is important to understand all of these elements in the context of the shopper and allow them to inform our choices. According to Ray Burke, the E.W. Kelley Chair of Business Administration and Founding Director of Indiana University's Customer Interface

---

41   Stone, Dorian and John Devine. "From Moments to Journeys: A Paradigm Shift in Customer Experience Excellence." McKinsey & Company, April 2013. http://csi.mckinsey.com/knowledge_by_topic/consumer_and_shopper_insights/consumer_experience_journey

Evolving from Product Warehouses to Retail Experiences | 145

Laboratory, "Today we know what consumers are buying, but not how they're buying."[42] By observing customers' paths through the store, Burke can determine the obstacles to purchase and identify what will stop consumers in their tracks. In the future, he expects that the market will see the same kind of gains from merchandizing optimization and product presentation that are now being achieved through price optimization techniques.

Virtual technologies now allow retailers and CPG manufacturers to design and test numerous scenarios without the cost of physical stores. Research can now be conducted in days instead of months, at a tenth of the cost by designing and testing multiple shopper scenarios and recording their shopping activities as they navigate through the virtual store, pick up and examine products, and place them in the basket.

Procter & Gamble has been using virtual technologies to conduct consumer research since 1997, having identified the technology as a way to develop its products and experiences to meet shopper's needs. According to P&G, the technology can "integrate consumer insights more efficiently" throughout a project's design process, reduce the time and cost it takes to develop the insights, and allow

---

42 "Shoppability: The Science of Shopping." Indiana University Kelley School of Business website.http://www.kelley.iu.edu/about/features/archive/fall_2007/shoppability1.html

P&G to ask more questions and probe for deeper insights in a shorter time frame.[43]

P&G is not alone. Kimberly-Clark Corp., Kellogg Co., Johnson and Johnson and others have used virtual technologies to conduct shopper research to guide their innovation efforts and help them design the right plan to win at the shelf. Both CPG manufacturers and retailers are using virtual simulations to effectively narrow down options and refine concepts so that the ultimate in-store test has a higher chance to succeed. According to Kimberly Senter, Director of Category Management at Unilever, "It saves us the embarrassment of a failed 20-store test."[44] Retailers like Wal-Mart, Sainsbury and others have also started using virtual technology to go beyond the data to understand shoppers, saving both time and helping to drive better merchandising plans and store designs in the process.

Designing the Retail Stage While Managing Complexity

Many retailers may feel that adopting a shopper-centric retail strategy is impossible because of the complexity of the retail environment. By their very nature, stores are very complex. An average grocery store holds between 50,000 and 60,000 SKUs that need to be configured on shelving and a space plan that fits the environment. Layer onto the complexity the constant churn of products, and it starts feel impossible to be able to define an experience that meets the needs of the local shopper.

Retailers need to use solutions that can combine assortment, category management and space planning into a single system can help manage the complexity of the product assortment, while managing the space effectively to create store specific or cluster-specific planograms. Many times, these functions are handled separately, which creates multiple rounds or rework or inefficiencies.

---

43 "Shaping Retail: The Use of Virtual Store Simulations in Marketing Research and Beyond." In-Store Marketing Institute, 2009.Page 18. http://kelley.iu.edu/CERR/files/09ISMI_VirtualRetailing.pdf

44 Ibid, page 10.

Retailers need to balance shopper preferences with a never-ending stream of new products, line extensions and promotions from their CPG partners. They need a solution that will allow them to define the products and subcategories and be able to manage their lifecycle over time. This "product life-cycle approach" helps manage the constant churn of products and ensure that the right products are available at the right place and time.

A master design can then be presented to shoppers virtually to test adjacencies, merchandising ideas and promotions in the context of an entire store. This allows retailers to assess the entire shopper journey from the moment they walk into the store until they check out. Without virtual technologies, ideas were either assessed through 2D paper drawings or physical tests in pilot stores. This made the testing cost prohibitive, time consuming, and risky to attempt novel designs. Virtual testing can help retailers design the right experience for their shoppers before spending significant time or capital to make it a reality.

Rules should then be formalized based on shopper understanding to be able to facilitate the translation of an assortment into a space plan for different retail environments. The solution allows retailers to use rules to adapt planograms by adjusting allocated space for the category to the store size and format, changing shelves and fixtures to adapt to the point-of-sale furniture and align with the local assortment. This can be done locally or from a central location while being compliant with the consumer decision tree and expected overall business performance. New variants can be generated in minutes instead working days to generate them manually.

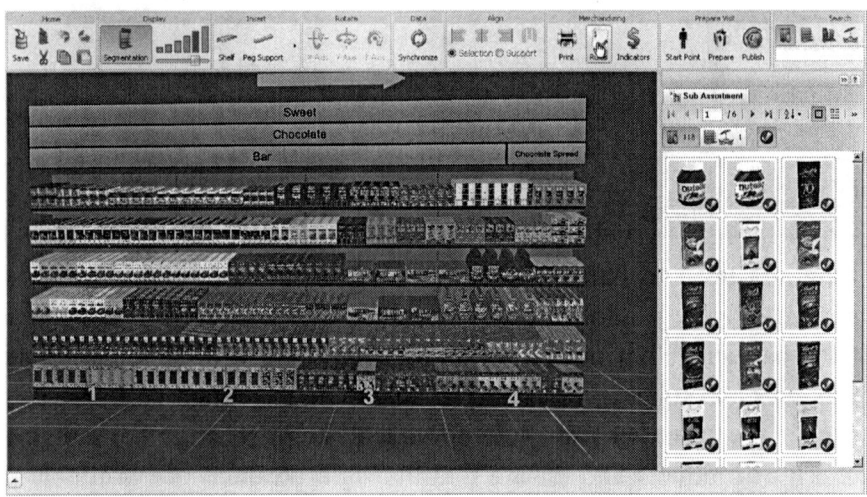

An integrated assortment, merchandising, and space management solution allows different teams to focus on the retail experience. Retailers can create an environment where shoppers can find the products they are looking for, successfully navigate through the store, and enjoy it. This requires specific attention to adjacencies designed around how the shopper thinks, creating the right signage and wayfinding, and creating the right brand experience. This is essential as retailers seek different ways to create experiences to combat the effects of showrooming and other pressures.

Going the Last Mile to Delight Shoppers

Ultimately, execution at the point of sale is critical for a retailer. A delightful shopping experience, brand equity consistency, and operational quality are achievable if sufficient care is taken to adapt master planograms to fit the local retail environment.

Creating planograms with 3D tools can avoid many of the operational issues found in store, accelerate store set-ups, and improve operational compliance. It is common for a corporate- or regional-level planogram team to get a lot of negative feedback from store employees because their carefully-configured planograms didn't work in execution. It's often because the planogram team was trying to use 2D planning tools to figure out how something would work in the real world.

As an example, it can be difficult to determine how many blister packs will fit on a peg hook unless you know the exact physical dimensions of the package, the exact position of the peg hook and even the clearance needed so a consumer can take one with their hand. In addition, irregularly shaped objects like a DVD player that indicate a 13-inch depth but do not account for the space the electrical cord sticks out can create significant operational issues. The corporate team has to do additional work, and the stores are left with merchandise that can't be displayed properly.[45]

In addition, creating mounting instructions in 3D takes the guesswork out of translating planograms. Perfect Shelf 3DEXPERIENCE from Dassault Systèmes provides the ability to generate the mounting instructions in multiple languages in a single click. Retailers using this solution have reported between 30% and 60% shorter store set times. It was easy to see how fixtures were supposed to be set up and where items were supposed to go. Compliance rates were significantly improved as a result.

Store managers can then focus their operations on delivering the right consumer experience instead of struggling with executing store designs. Time can be spent on customer engagement, operational excellence, expediting the shopping process and managing issues. The design of a store can help eliminate the issues like out-of-stocks, which frustrate shoppers, and focus employees on delighting them instead.

---

45 "Perfect Shelf to Design Real Shopping Experience." Desktop Engineering, September 20, 2012. http://www.deskeng.com/virtual_desktop/?p=6207

Evolve or Be Commoditized

Virtual technologies have taken these risks out designing shopper experiences by allowing retailers and CG manufacturers to co-create and test multiple ideas in days instead of months, at a tenth of the cost and effort. Many leading CPG companies and retailers are using virtual solutions to better understand the shopping experience, explore retail strategies to combat the pressures of commoditization, and validate these new designs with consumers in a short period of time. History is littered with retail chains that have failed to evolve. Now there is a way to accelerate this evolution from a product warehouse into a shopping experience that delights consumers and meets their needs.

Eric Seiberling is the Consumer Packaged Goods and Retail Industry Global Marketing Director for Dassault Systemes, the 3DEXPERIENCE Company, provider of virtual universes to imagine sustained innovations. Its solutions are designed to accelerate better, faster, smart innovation for the CPG, Packaging and Retail Industries. For more information: www.3ds.com/CPG.

SECTION FIVE
DIGITAL

CHAPTER 14

The Emergence of Digital Sampling

By Larry Burns

Digital sampling has been a viable promotion for several years. But the time is right for digital tactics to ramp up their share of the sampling business. Why? Simply because consumers are spending more and more time online via PCs, tablets and smartphones. It only makes sense that product sampling would flourish in these environments. That's where people are nowadays.

Online sampling starts with strategically placed media – a banner ad or button – on the website of a retailer, brand, or publisher. It is a call to action. As such, consumers actively engage with the product by selecting the product sample. In a practical sense, such a request indicates an actual interest in that sample. After all, consumers need to provide their name and address, making them travel partway along the Path to Purchase. Hence, they are more likely to convert to a purchase of the product after the sample arrives if their experience lives up to the expectations set in the offer that prompted their action.

The science of consumer decision-making shows that personal experience trumps everything else as an influence on choice. People may be mistrustful of advertising, but they do trust their own senses. Sampling creates that personal experience. No other promotional tactic is as powerful as a direct experience with the brand.

These fundamental precepts are particularly true when the product's characteristics themselves include a high trial hurdle (for example, belief in concentrated detergent), when the brand has a definitive usage niche (for example, adult incontinence remedies), when the brand has a unique audience (for example, African-Americans targeted for Soft Sheen), and so on. All types of sampling may work for these objectives, but online sampling is a very effective subset for the sampling of categories that have characteristics such as these.

The science of consumer decision-making also tells us that a product recommendation from a trusted friend is the second most important purchase influencer. As we now understand, and what many brands measure, the social sharing phenomena is magnified online with clear indications that a successful sampling program should take full advantage of inherently being a highly social and viral activity. When a person has a positive brand experience that they consider worthwhile, they are very likely to spread the word and tell their friends.

Social by Nature
One key advantage for online sampling in the 21st century is clear: It helps brands put samples in places where people are going to be – such as on Facebook and other social networks. Companies have scored some success in doing so because offering a bit of information and answering a few questions is seen as a fair value exchange. For example, to qualify to receive a sample, you may have to "like" the brand offering it. That is referred to as "like-gating." In other words, you can only participate in this offer if you come through the gate; "liking" a brand is very small hurdle.

A few years ago, Facebook and YouTube were used by Seattle's Best Coffee to conduct an e-sampling program surrounding the launch of an easier way to define the product's "flavor system." Consumers were invited to participate in an entire 24-hour Second City Improvisation webcast and take a test on the strengths of coffee they preferred while on the site. One vendor, StartSampling, was so impressed with the potential of integrating samples into such promotions that it built application interfaces to most of the social media sites. They report an ever increasing usage of all manner of social media outreach programs to consumers, many of which are successfully integrating sampling programs.

Return on Investment

When considering the ROI of any version of e-sampling program, it's important to recognize the significant social and viral impact. As of 2013, they have not been integrated into the ROI calculations of many brands. Let us assume that people try and "like" a sample. By sharing their experience, other people (their friends) become aware of the brand. These friends' subsequent purchases don't equal zero. While it's a lower percentage of purchase that is seen among those who had the chance to actually try a sample, it's definitely not zero. Yet nearly all the ROI models fail to take this into account.

The ROI on e-sampling has been demonstrated to be very solid for more than a decade. According to surveys conducted by StartSampling, nearly 85% of consumers across one specific manufacturer's programs reported they were "completely" or "very" satisfied with their product sample. The average "top two box" purchase intent across all these manufacturer programs was nearly 82% (81.8%). This suggests a high level of involvement and quality media placement. This data was based on over 48,500 consumer interviews across all completed specific manufacturer programs. In fact:

- The average conversion (first purchase) after sample trial across all this manufacturer's e-sampling programs was 47.5%, which compares very favorably to the overall average of 33% across all sampled products[1].

- These programs also enjoyed a large viral opportunity. Some 42.7% of all manufacturer samplers reported they would *definitely* recommend products they have tried on (retailer).com to a friend. This viral aspect extended the reach of these campaigns well beyond the e-samplers alone.

Zero Moment of Truth

The traditional Path to Purchase consists of Stimulus (pre-store: advertising), First Moment of Truth (at shelf), and Second Moment of Truth (at home: consumers decide whether to repeat purchase). There is substantial evidence that today's Path to Purchase begins with a new Stimulus called the Zero Moment of Truth[2].

The ZMOT signifies the emergence of significant search and online engagement prior to shopping. Product buyers or targets found online rely on their social network for input. One very influential thing within ZMOT is the product "reviews" that people post. Digital sampling programs provide an opportunity for people to write about and talk about their experiences. They clearly do so, and hence sampling contributes quite directly to important information sought at the ZMOT.

Free vs. Paid Media

In the digital sampling space, there are three broad types of media: owned, paid, and earned. There is a clear difference between online sampling via free media and paid media.

It's common to find a sampling program for a CPG company on a brand's own site, or on the marketing platform associated with the company's brands; for example, "Right at Home" with SC Johnson, "My Very Best _____" for Nestle, or "Home Made Simple" for Procter & Gamble. Samples can and are being integrated into the brand's marketing platform within the online space via email campaigns, social media efforts (Facebook, Twitter, etc.), e-newsletters, or whatever forms this use of "owned media" is. Sampling is integrated to take full advantage of these owned media assets, which can be considered "free media," thereby increasing the overall ROI of the sampling activity.

For "paid media" – for example, banner ads – what is very valuable online is the ability to track activity. Let's say a company is making a media purchase on a particular ad network or a particular site such as ESPN. They just have to tag the URLs put into each of the ad units, which is on its way to becoming standard practice. As the program is running, automated reporting monitors can tell how many people are coming to the landing page or micro-site from each unique media placement to submit their order for a sample. Companies can then adapt media in real time to meet their objectives. This provides an alternative to the lament that "the creative isn't working" or "I'm not getting the conversion rates I wanted." It also answers several obvious questions: What is the conversion in terms of the people who arrive at the site versus those who actually place an order? What percent of them are coming from, say, ESPN versus Oprah?

Another component of online sampling is having access to a definitive electronic closed loop of behavioral research given the vast retailer databases that now exist – known as "Big Data." For example, a company provides a sample to a list of shoppers who are a "known" set of shoppers. It's possible to read what those shoppers buy via analysis of frequent shopper card data.

As we move further into this decade, we anticipate the increased use of credit card transaction data as a source of consumer data as well. In addition, there are other kinds of programs such as Walmart Direct™ that enable the retailer to first precisely target multiple groups and then track purchase results among some ~50 million households of purchase data. A major advantage of online sampling is reaching households with a particular sample and monitoring the actual purchasing behavior later on.

How It Works
Let's look at how consumers request samples online with a standard form that currently exists in the retailer marketplace.

Once consumers online take action to engage with the sample offer by "clicking" – saying, in effect, they want to obtain the sample – they are brought to single-page registration form where they provide their name and address. They are next asked some simple questions: brand usage, how often they use the category, etc., Consumers are then asked specifically if they can be contacted later for their opinions on the samples they try. In 2013, often half of the participants said YES. Since there is a value exchange, people are happy to comply and offer their opinions.

Consumers are then shown an order confirmation page and a brief delivery timeframe is set to manage their expectations. Finally, a "Thank You" page is displayed that ends the interaction and offers the sampler a chance to further engage. There often are links for Twitter, Facebook and other social media options included. Samples are shipped via the postal system in co-branded packaging to generate awareness and trial for both the brand and the retail partner. For a small retailer, the sample may be shipped in a customer's brand packaging, including a "Compliments of" mention in the address block.

Challenges

Among the many considerations to successful digital sampling, a few challenges stand out:

- Media to bring people to the sample offer is still typically bought on an impression basis

- Relying on "impression delivery" as a metric of success has often not driven the desired action of selecting a sample to try

- Media budgets, based in impression delivery, can exhaust well before meeting the brand objective of having X million samples ordered.

Bottom line result: Companies either reduce the volume of samplers reached or believe that e-sampling really doesn't work well.

But the reality is that many programs are simply not conducted effectively. Media buying for *sample request programs* has not been optimized, and to date overall sampling spend in the digital market has been negatively impacted.

To remedy this situation, one vendor, StartSampling, implemented a solution that conducts e-sampling programs on a Cost-Per-Acquisition (CPA) basis. The solution guarantees a fixed budget and accelerated orders. Its Sample Request Media campaigns are sold as a CPA model. As such, the focus is on scale and efficiency. This approach offers guaranteed pay for performance, and it is slowly becoming an accepted practice. Clients that use campaigns of this type have included Kraft, ConAgra, Kimberly-Clark, Procter & Gamble, among others.

Summary

Personal experience is the best motivator of behavior change. So, giving a consumer the chance to have a personal experience via a sample is the first step toward a purchase. Program success can be enhanced when a serious effort is made to amplify the potential advocacy of samplers pleased with their discovery. Brands need to actively find ways to amplify these sampler's voices by making it easy for them to share and talk about their experiences. That approach drives their friends to listen and perhaps become interested, too.

Online sampling is growing quickly as an important tactic in a manufacturer's overall sampling strategy. They are starting to spend resources and think about how to integrate logical sampling programs from both the "pull/request" mode and the "push" mode into their overall retail and merchandising planning cycle.

For example, a manufacturer with a rewards program can reward their elite members by providing them with samples related to the merchandising events going on. In other words, sampling can be used as *reward* for being a good consumer and shopper as well as its traditional role of generating trial. More and more, the tactic of sampling is being thought of as a strategy that can be deployed to enhance rewards. Samples increase the shoppers' good feelings about a retailer, whose goal is to get a larger share of their wallet in the store. The manufacturer's goal is to get consumers to buy more products – or a certain product versus a competitive product – in the store. A sample helps connect these shoppers with both the retailer and the brand, and serves to enhance these crucial relationships.

> ### *How to Choose an Online Sampling Vendor*
>
> Companies looking to offer e-sampling programs should select a vendor with the following qualifications:
>
> **Solid Track Record** – Years of experience managing e-sampling programs for high-profile retailers and manufacturers
>
> **Experienced Team** – Hands-on practitioners who know the details of managing a successful e-sampling promotion
>
> **Outstanding Controls** – Expert media source tracking, real time reporting, inventory management, state-of-the-art fulfillment center, "earned media" controls, and brand peace of mind
>
> **Superior Market Research** – Benchmarks against category norms (by retailer), plus years of experience in market research
>
> **Appropriate Scale to Deliver Competitive Prices** – Since the U.S. Postal Service is a large cost driver for delivering samples ordered online, the vendor should have ongoing processes to continually seek both cost savings and program efficiency
>
> **Focus** – Sampling should be the primary focus of the vendor. In today's marketing landscape, far too many entities are offering "sampling solutions" without a true appreciation of all that is involved to deliver success.

Larry Burns is president of StartSampling, an online promotional marketing services company focused exclusively on product sampling. For more information: www.StartSamplingInc.com

References
1. Based on StartSampling Retailer Network e-Sampling database representing over 500 programs and results from over 700,000 completed surveys
2. ZMOT is a term fully explained by Google in their e-book "Winning the Zero Moment of Truth" (2011). They note that the first use of the term was in a Symphony/IRI Group Report in October 2009, "Zero Moment of Truth: Redefining the Consumer Decision-Making Process."

CHAPTER 15

The Multi-Channel Shopper and the Importance of Consistency

By Steve Cole

Today, driven by the Internet and mobile technology, almost every shopper is a multi-channel shopper based on their preferences to conduct research and make purchases across a variety of channels and platforms including websites, mobile applications, and in-store. As a result, the product information consumers receive comes not just from traditional advertising but from a diverse array of ever-expanding sources including manufacturer and retailer websites, third-party websites, blogs, social media, and mobile applications.

Findings from various studies are compelling:

- Three quarters of U.S. Internet users research grocery and personal care products online.

- More than 70 percent of shoppers would like electronic delivery of advertising inserts.

- Over 80 percent of shoppers make their purchase decision before they leave home.

- The number of U.S. consumers with smartphones will more than double from 93.1 million at the end of 2011 to 192.4 million by 2016. At that time, 58.5% of the population will have the devices.

- 84 percent of smartphone users integrate their mobile phone into their grocery shopping journey in some way.

- 62 percent of smartphone users have made a purchase via a mobile device.

- Over 50 percent of smartphone owners use the device while in the store to guide their purchases.

- 73 percent of shoppers prefer to reference their smartphones while in store rather than ask a sales associate for help.

Manufacturers are responding by creating sophisticated, interactive experiences supplemented by mobile apps and social media. Time-pressed shoppers use these resources to learn about the products, get accurate nutritional information and plan menus.

Influencing Brand Purchases

Similarly, retailers are communicating with shoppers through their own websites, offering product samples, menu planning, nutritional advice and, more recently, publishing digital versions of their weekly circulars online. In addition to circulars going online, a growing number of progressive retailers have moved their inventory online, allowing consumers to research products before coming to the store or ordering online for in-store pickup.

Even as manufacturers and retailers discover new ways to build and maintain relationships with shoppers, consumers are becoming more independent and are finding innovative online resources to support their shopping. Some examples:

- Alice.com provides a simple tool that helps consumers maintain their inventory of staple products.

- Mercatus Technologies' Concierge system allows shoppers to build a list and then locate the item in the store.

- FoodEssentials.com identifies allergens and allows comparison of manufacturer product claims.

- CalorieCount.com focuses on providing nutrition information to the diet-conscious.

- Blogs and social networks foster a dynamic interchange of product information, reviews, shopping tips, and menu ideas.

Blogs in particular have evolved significantly over the last 18 months, especially the coupon blogs and the so-called "mommy" blogs. They now must be a critical part of any brand owner's marketing plans, although because of their diversity they add greatly to the challenge of consistency.

There is still a fair amount of fragmentation with a large number of blogs addressing very specialized interests. There are blogs for new moms, blogs for gluten-free foods for celiac disease sufferers, blogs for the elderly, and others.

They've become channels for the marketers to communicate with those specific audiences. But here is the challenge: Because these channels are so diverse, a brand owner has a difficult job getting the information about individual products to all the bloggers in a consistent way and on time for the article that blogger is writing.

New product introductions provide great opportunities to partner with bloggers. New food or health and beauty care items targeted toward a niche audience will often be soft-launched through the blogs first before the mainstream media. This enables the marketer to build a core audience early on at a relatively low cost, and with relatively low risk.

Taken together, these new sources of information offer a myriad of opportunities to connect with shoppers. But they also present brand owners and retailers with some significant challenges, not the least of which is ensuring the information the consumer encounters is consistent, complete, and accurate, regardless of its source.

Mickey Alam Khan, editor-in-chief at *Mobile Marketer*, wrote that the multi-channel shopper expects a "frictionless ... searching, shopping, browsing or buying experience [that is] devoid of hurdles or pain points." To satisfy that expectation, consistency across all brand-to-consumer interactions is necessary. It must be the same information, with the same package design, in the same size, and with the same product code, whether the product is examined on the shelf, in advertising, at a kiosk, on a website, on a smart phone app, or on a nutritionist's blog. Consistency is not only crucial, it is expected.

Catering to Consumer Preferences
Today's consumer is looking for a rich description of products including images and ingredient lists, as well as extended information such as nutrition, allergens, and directions. She may want detailed information to answer specific questions before she adds a product to the shopping list: How many calories? Is it gluten-free? How much sodium per serving? What is the correct dosage for a child? This information must be readily available, accurate, and up-to-date.

Retailers have to make sure they are showing the same image and the same information about a product regardless of the channel in which they are publishing it. The shopper expects that the brand will be consistently represented. When it is not, it undermines the shopper's confidence either in the brand itself, or in the retailer.

For brand owners, a crisis point has been reached: Their brands are online and often in the hands of someone they don't know. They must take steps – sooner rather than later – to manage their images and content actively to ensure that they get the proper product image and information to not only their retail partners, but also to the many independent websites, blogs and mobile app providers that are offering their own solutions and points-of-view. CPG manufacturers have to find a way to provide comprehensive product details across entire categories and, as product details change, offer immediate updates.

Three best practices in accomplishing this are:

- **Leverage a consolidated product database**: To promote the accuracy, efficiency, and availability of product content, brand marketers can leverage a consolidated database for product information either in-house or provided and hosted by a third party. By leveraging a one-stop-shop for product content, marketers can save time in their daily tasks, ensure that the information they provide vendors and partners is consistent and accurate, and drive efficiencies.

- **Commit to constant updates**: Brand marketers should commit to internal processes or a third-party resource that helps guarantee product information is constantly updated to maintain the validity of the data.

- *Promote scalable distribution:* Like most business processes, it can be best to automate the distribution of product content to promote efficiencies and reduce the likelihood of human error. With new channels for product information popping up each day such as websites, social media, blogs, mobile applications, etc., it's important to focus on scalability in a distribution strategy.

The brand owner has few options when it comes to delivering this information in an efficient, uniform and scalable manner. Delegating the task to an internal department or an advertising agency which must identify and then connect with every website or blog is rarely practical or affordable. Allowing independent websites and social media mavens to seek out information on their own wherever and whenever they can, and then present possibly inaccurate product images and information, can have serious repercussions for the brand.

The do-it-yourself model is not as easy as it looks. The product information and images, as well as logistics information, tend to be scattered across the organization. It can be a real treasure hunt to find the accurate information and images that they actually want to publish. It becomes more challenging when you extend that problem from one package to collecting and maintaining the product information and images for potentially hundreds or thousands of products.

Distribution of the product information and images is another part of the problem: How to get it to all of the people who need it. This list may include really large retailers like Target, Safeway and CVS, e-retailers like Amazon and eBay, search engines like Google, and the mommy blogs. It becomes a major challenge for individual brand owners to do it themselves.

Driving Profits with Effective Digital Solutions

Another, more complete, solution that is gaining traction is third-party services that are experts at collecting images and information from manufacturers, standardizing the formats and then distributing that content to retailers and other users. For a brand owner, this single-source solution creates a near-seamless, cost-effective routine process for distributing content to his constituents. Retailers and web-based information sources can be confident that the images and information they provide to consumers is complete, accurate and available to them whenever they need it.

Companies like Gladson have the processes and the economies of scale to build these databases and maintain them consistently, along with all the connections with the consumers of the information: the retailers, e-retailers, search engines, blogs, couponing companies, and so on.

This means having the work flow in place with people who are skilled at taking the right images, and making sure those images are of high quality so they meet the needs of the customers or the publishers who are going to use those images. It also means knowing how to classify the information that we get about the product, how to categorize and effectively code information about the product so it can be used by websites and marketers effectively, and doing it in a way that is scalable.

Shoppers are learning about and selecting the products they buy from a rapidly growing universe of sources. It is essential that they see consistent and accurate information about each product no matter where they look. The multi-channel shopper expects nothing less.

The challenge for brand owners and retailers is that technology is moving quickly and consumers are moving with that technology. They are not only actively seeking out information about the products that they buy now, but the media that they are using is rapidly evolving, and their expectations are increasing almost every day. The foundation of keeping up is having really good product information to start with. If you don't have that strong foundation, then you are not going to be able to keep up.

Steve Cole is the Chief Marketing Officer of Gladson, a provider of syndicated consumer packaged goods (CPG) product information and services for manufacturers, retailers, wholesalers and brokers. For more information: www.gladson.com.

Sources:

- Three quarters of U.S. Internet users research grocery and personal care products online. (SOURCE: "The New Shopper," Carat & Microsoft Advertising, March 2010)

- More than 70 percent of shoppers would like electronic delivery of advertising inserts. (SOURCE: "The Evolution of Circulars," Nielsen Q.4, 2011)

- Over 80 percent of shoppers make their purchase decision before they leave home. (SOURCE: "Zero Moment of Truth," Times and Trends Report, Oct. 2009, IRI/Symphony)

- The number of U.S. consumers with smartphones will more than double from 93.1 million at the end of 2011 to 192.4 million by 2016. At that time, 58.5% of the population will have the devices. (SOURCE: eMarketer.com, April 8, 2012, citing eMarketer estimates.)

- 84 percent of smartphone users integrate their mobile phone into their grocery shopping journey in some way. (SOURCE: Research by the instant.ly blog, Jan. 13, 2013.)

- Sixty-two percent of smartphone users have made a purchase via a mobile device. (SOURCE: Mobile Commerce Daily, 2/14/2011, citing Adobe survey.)

- Over 50 percent of smartphone owners use the device while in the store to guide their purchases. (SOURCE: Pew American & Internet Life Project 2012.)

- Seventy-three percent of shoppers prefer to reference their smartphones while in the store rather than ask a sales associate for help.(SOURCE: Internet Retailer, Dec. 2010, reporting on study by Accenture.)

- Print advertising ad revenues have dropped 60% over seven years with 27 consecutive quarters of year-on-year declines.(SOURCE: MediaPost News, May 22, 2013, citing the Newspaper Association of America.)

CHAPTER 16

The Emerging Mobile Coupon Ad Unit Standards

By Adam Lavine

Marketing and consumer packaged goods (CPG) companies know mobile coupons hold huge potential for them, but they simply don't know where to start. Faced with a bewildering array of choices, companies struggle to connect the dots on how mobile coupons can drive redemption, given grocery's reliance on red laser scanning technologies. Additionally, many executives are somewhat distrustful of the easily-shared screen grab nature of the device. They don't know how to integrate mobile coupons into traditional point of sale (POS), the most effective form of redemption measurement.

In 2012, the Mobile Marketing Association (MMA) launched a forward-looking initiative to create a Mobile Coupon Ad Units Standard, or MoCAUS for short. The goal of the MoCAUS committee is to establish a shared set of terminology, measurements, and ad unit sizes around the creation, distribution, and redemption of mobile coupons. The MMA is uniquely positioned for such an effort, having deep mobile knowledge, experience and credibility, as well a membership of agencies, ad networks, CPG companies, and mobile technology providers.

Since this initiative was launched, it's attracted strong industry interest and participation. Participating companies include Valpak, Yahoo!, Catalina, Inmar, Sprint-Nextel, ISIS, Spotzot, Univision, Tribune, FunMobility and many others. Mobile coupons are uniquely positioned to close the loop between mobile media spend and a retail redemption event.

Consumers are spending 12% of their screen time with their mobile device – an average of 200 daily screen views – and take their mobile phones shopping in ways that are increasingly integrated into the retail experience. Despite these facts, average mobile media spend remains a paltry 1.7% of total marketing budgets. Mobile coupons are poised to change that, and unlock huge benefits for advertisers, retailers and consumers alike.

Renowned mobile researcher and consultant Tomi Ahonen calls mobile "The 7th Mass Media" after print, recording, cinema, radio, TV, and the internet. It's also the fastest growing media type ever, and the first personal mass medium. Mobile is the only form of media that is always carried, always connected, has a built-in payment channel, and makes the physical world interactive with the tap of a screen. Mobile has the most accurate and precise audience data, because a mobile device is almost always used by the same person, especially phones (as opposed to tablets), which are the mobile devices carried in-store. The Pew American Life Project survey of 2,277 adults found that 31% of them prefer to be contacted by advertisers on mobile phones rather than other mediums.

Mobile consumers want to be reached with the right deal at the right time, and mobile media is far less costly than traditional forms of advertising. So why aren't more advertisers and retailers embracing mobile as their core approach to advertising and Customer Relationship Management (CRM)? Why do advertisers instead continue to pour millions of dollars into arguably less effective forms of media?

The answer lies in the perceived and actual complexity of executing and measuring effective mobile coupons, promotions, and brand loyalty initiatives. And that's where the MMA Mobile Coupon Ad Unit Standard comes in. The standard is designed to flexibly create and launch both retailer-driven store mobile coupons as well as CPG / manufacturer-driven mobile coupon campaigns. It does this by creating a standardized mobile coupon "Ad Unit" that is flexible about how it can be discovered, clipped and redeemed, while having simple, attractive, and easy-to-implement creative standards.

Mobile Coupon Ad Units can be discovered in-store via signs, receipts, on-pack or circulars. This is done in a variety of ways: Scannable QR codes, SMS short codes or simple URLs. Mobile Coupon Ad Units can also be connected to traditional Free-Standing Inserts (FSIs) in similar fashion. Clip Units are also designed to be connected to mobile display ads, opening up intriguing targeting possibilities such as geo-targeted ad buys near a retail location (or competitor's retail locations).

Once discovered, Mobile Coupon Clip Units have a variety of clip options: Inbox Clip via SMS or email, AppClip to digital wallets such as Apple's Passbook, or ID Clip to a loyalty or payment card. It is this last form of clipping that has the potential to unlock and revolutionize CPG-driven coupons because it integrates into a well-trodden path created by existing industry players like Inmar, Catalina, Valassis and Coupons Inc. Furthermore, this eliminates the need for red laser scanning, and also reduces the exposure to fraud. That's because these mobile coupons can be issued on a 1:1 basis as they are linked to a consumer's loyalty card.

The Mobile Coupon Ad Unit addresses these myriad clipping choices by "chicklets" which are small buttons that can be embedded in the mobile coupon on a campaign-by-campaign basis. An in-store campaign for a store coupon with optical scanning at POS might call for a Inbox chicklet and a Passbook chicklet. A major media buy for a CPG product might just call for an ID Clip to a loyalty card. This flexibility means the Mobile Coupon Ad Unit can be relevant and useful to a broad variety of products and promotional situations, and work equally well for CPG and store coupons alike.

Once clipped, the final issue of validation remains. The Coupon Ad Unit Standard calls for a simple Transaction ID that can be associated with the digital clearing and validation process that already exists in the industry. This Transaction ID will also enable added services such as text reminders and geo-notifications for coupons that have not yet been used, as well as coupon clipboxes that can be integrated into mobile apps and websites.

Trish Mueller, the CMO of The Home Depot (and an active MMA member) said in a recent talk that her mobile strategy includes always looking through a customer lens, as well as continual, agile testing and learning. Now is a great time to get involved with the MMA Mobile Coupon Ad Unit initiative, and be able to learn from being involved with the process of testing and iterating around the new proposed standards. People interested in participating can contact committees@mmaglobal.com, or coupons@funmobility.com.

Adam Lavine is the Chairman of the Mobile Marketing Association's Mobile Coupon Ad Unit Standards Committee. He is also the Chief Executive Officer of FunMobility, a mobile brand loyalty solutions provider. For more information: www.funmobility.com.

CHAPTER 17

Five Keys to Securing the Future of Mobile Coupons

By Wade Allen

While the majority of the spend on coupons is still for paper-based media, digital forms are rapidly gaining traction and marketers are closely monitoring progress in mobile technologies.

When the point-of-sale infrastructure at retail is sufficiently built up, there will be an aggressive transition to mobile. But that may take as long as five years. Accepting mobile coupons at the retail point-of-sale (POS) remains cumbersome, if not impossible, without a sizable investment of dollars in hardware and software. However, growth in other digital coupon forms will continue.

Because print-at-home coupons must be rendered on paper before they can be used for a discount, many don't regard them as digital. Instead they will call them "internet coupons." However, since their distribution is digital, and they are the biggest component of electronic discounts today, they should be considered as digital.

Then there are the load-to-card discounts, which are now seeing rapid growth. But this requires some infrastructure investment for retailers, and makes the consumer do some preparation, such as inputting their loyalty card number, before using them.

Meanwhile, the wait goes on for the widespread adoption of mobile coupons. Consumers prefer the relative ease of using these discounts direct from their smart phones compared to clipping, organizing and presenting paper coupons. Once established, the clearing of mobile coupons would be entirely electronic and seamless, making it easier for the coupon industry.

To reach that mobile couponing future, there are five issues that must be confronted and overcome:

Integration

The biggest obstacle is the integration of the POS system with the mobile device. Today only 5-10% of food, drug and mass grocery stores — these are retailers selling perishables and high consumption products in addition to other products — allow true mobile couponing.

They struggle with the ability to scan a barcode and get it into the POS system, which requires a line-of-sight scanner, or an otherwise upgraded front-end scanner, to read codes off phones. The cost per lane can be $600 for one line-of-sight scanner, although a retail chain buying great quantities will obtain cost efficiencies that will reduce the cost to the $300-400 range. Even at the lower cost, this means a multi-million dollar investment for a large chain, with more costs involved in upgrading software.

Operational Efficiency

Besides the retailers' ability to accept the coupons, there must be refinements in the way the discounts are presented on the phone. Currently, mobile coupons are shown one at a time, and it is uncertain whether any given customer will bring up the code on the mobile screen before the cashier is ready to scan it. Most customers will present several coupons in a grocery transaction, so there is a challenge of creating a smart barcode that combines all those coupon codes into one that allows it to be one scan and done, as opposed to multiple scans off a phone, with the customer searching for each barcode and slowing down the checkout line.

Before couponing can move to an all-mobile solution, retailers and other players in the industry need to figure out how to handle that operational inefficiency.

Electronic Clearing

A third concern is the electronic clearing of these mobile coupons. Currently, the coupon infrastructure is based on the paper-based system, where boxes of coupons are shipped to locations around the country to be counted and scanned to create a paper trail based on what has actually come across the POS system. The clearing houses that represent the brand and the retailer then settle up to make that appropriate exchange of dollars.

When the industry moves to an all-electronic system, there is investment needed on the part of the clearing houses, as well as trust in the electronic clearing coming from the retailer and then going to the brand. The numbers have to align; that is, the data that is being passed between those two entities has to be the same. The clearing houses have to be in sync from an electronic standpoint.

The industry is moving in that direction, but it isn't clear whether that investment has been made on the clearing side of the coupon industry yet.

Security

The fourth key to advancing mobile couponing is to secure the system from fraud. In a mobile environment today, the barcode on the phone needs to be saved in some way, whether on a browser or in an app. Then there has to be a means to expire that coupon. With paper coupons, the cashier takes it out of the shopper's possession so it can't be used in another transaction or at another store. But for mobile devices, there are still questions about how the expiration of the coupon will work. How does the industry make sure there isn't massive malredemption or misredemption, and how does it limit consumers from gaming the mobile barcodes?

Systems could be implemented where the code on the phone is swiped or tapped and then disappears. But there has to be a consensus by couponing experts in the industry on how that is going to be delivered and displayed. One possibility is a time limit of 15-60 minutes from when the mobile coupon is activated to when it expires. But consumers will need to be educated about that so they don't activate the coupon too early, especially if they are standing in a long checkout line.

Money Talks

There has to be a conscious shift of trust and dollars. Today brand manufacturers and retailers all think a lot about mobile, and all they think it is a great and sexy thing. They want to move in that direction, but dollars speak louder than words. When they invest in putting coupons into a mobile promotion, as opposed to a freestanding insert (FSI), a print-at-home or a load-to-card solution, that's when we will see that tipping point.

It's like a Catch 22: The infrastructure has to be built before the dollars will be committed. Retailers are very astute and they understand that these coupons need a firm platform to land on before manufacturers will move their money over to digital.

At that point, brands will vote with their dollars, and there will be a sizable shift into digital and away from the traditional paper coupon. That will happen in the next five years, but paper coupons will always be a coupon delivery vehicle. Direct mail, FSIs, Valpak — these combined mailers are still going to be tactics that people are going to keep in their arsenal. But digital will become a much more sizable player when brands ultimately make the shift with their dollars.

Digital is the future. It will not be the only tool in the toolbox, but it will be a very impactful tool in the next three to five years. At that time, the brands and retailers that have invested in the technology will be in a much better position than those who have not.

Wade Allen is President, CouponFactory, a digital and mobile coupon provider specializing in promotional cloud-based technology for brands and retailers. For more information: www.couponfactory.com and wade.allen@couponfactory.com.

CHAPTER 18

Coupon Processing Stuck in the '80s

By Jon Robertson

Years ago, before electronic check validation became a standard procedure, retailers were vulnerable to fraudulent check-writing and bounced checks. They had to depend on cashiers to refer to printed lists of known passers of bad checks. It would take weeks to know whether a particular check had bounced or a fraudulent check had been accepted.

Automated services were launched by various companies to minimize the retailers' losses, changing the way consumers use and retailers accept checks. Starting with negative check databases, which enable a software solution to do the look up-and identify the potential bad check, the cashier was freed up to service customers more quickly while the system did the work to block bad checks.

But technology needed to advance further. These initial check verification services were not real-time solutions. Consequently, they stopped many customers who had valid checks but, for past reasons, had been placed on the negative file. Non-real time, negative check files therefore often translated into negative customer service.

Eventually, an electronic check approval process was introduced to the market. The check could now be scanned at checkout and validated in real time against other known fraudulent checks. Electronic check approval solutions gained in popularity and functionality as time passed. Soon the checks were validated, approved for deposit, and endorsed "for deposit only." The solution has advanced to the point where they can tell the retailer if there is an open active account at that bank and if the check is likely to clear. Status messages such as "closed account," "insufficient funds," "stop payment" or "invalid account" can help determine if a check or ACH transaction will be good.

These capabilities were made possible by the fact that the solutions were *real time.* Customer service levels improved dramatically. Although the use of debit cards spread in the meantime, diminishing the number of paper checks tendered, many retailers continue to accept paper checks. This occurs without creating a drag on customer service, or the security and productivity of the front end. They received their necessary dose of automation, and have a continued role in the twenty-first century.

When we fast-forward to today, we see that the same manual, fraud-prone environment *still exists* for the handling of paper coupons at the point of sale (POS). The retailer incurs labor and other associated costs for store-level accounting, or leaves open the opportunity for coupons to be redeemed improperly. In effect, today's manual process requires the cashier to control and stop coupon fraud. It depends on *cashiers* to ensure that the proper products are being purchased and that consumers have not passed expired coupons or other coupons that the retailer will have trouble getting reimbursed for by the manufacturers.

Furthermore, in the current '80's style process, there is virtually no accurate reporting for paper coupons. There is no practical way to verify after redemption what products were actually purchased, nor is there other data to help the retailer resolve costly disputes with the manufacturers. In summary, paper coupon processing is *still* plagued with virtually all the same problems once associated with manual control of check-cashing.

Joining the Twenty-First Century

Electronic real-time coupon validation will bring the retailer's coupon handling and payment processes, at last, into the digital age – with all of the associated benefits. A real-time electronic solution sees the contents of the entire basket and needs to intercept the scan of a paper coupon before the POS application can validate it. The scanned paper coupon data needs to be sent (as in the check world today) via a real-time service so the paper coupon can be validated. In addition to validating the paper coupon, the solution will need to check for fraud against a negative or positive master file. When a paper coupon cannot be validated against items purchased, or is identified as a fraudulent paper coupon, a customized message could be sent back to the POS in milliseconds.

Customer service for shoppers with coupons will be enhanced as much as it has been for the check-cashing customer. Cashiers will no longer need to be the coupon police, and manufactures will pay for all the coupons processed through an accurate electronic real-time solution.

This technology would provide these services for both paper and digital coupons. It sets the standard for the industry – much as electronic check validation did decades ago.

Costs of Staying Where We Are

Since most retailers do not validate at the family code level today or have other controls in place, paper coupons are inevitably tendered and accepted under the following circumstances:

- No family item purchased

- No company item purchased

- Insufficient quantity of promoted items purchased

- Expired coupons redeemed

- Fraudulent coupons redeemed.

All of these mis/malredemptions have a direct cost to the retailer and manufacturer. They are the basis of many of the coupon collection disputes and delayed payments between retailers and manufacturers.

Since many retailers do not have the needed controls in place at the POS, various levels of in-store cashier fraud can occur. Many of the coupon over-rides are simply the cashier trying to make the customer happy; without real-time messaging to the cashier, neither the customer nor the cashier can truly and fully understand why a coupon does not scan.

A second and more costly type of cashier fraud is due to the lack of store-level coupon accounting. With the cost being very high for the retailer to count the coupons at the store level, most retailers have simply eliminated store-level accounting. Store employees know that the back office has stopped counting coupons. They are using the POS t-log, rather than a physical count, as the record of coupons redeemed. Therefore, there is no way to account for differences between coupons scanned at the checkout and coupons redeemed for payment from the manufacturer. Without store-level accounting, cashiers can reduce any transaction they wish by merely scanning a high-value coupon multiple times.

Real-time electronic validation will stop misredemption and save the retailer the cost of this type of cashier fraud—without the retailer incurring the cost of store-level accounting.

The issues of counterfeiting and fraudulent coupons have a direct cost again to both manufacturers and retailers. An important data point noted is that counterfeit and fraudulent coupons are accepted by the retailer 75% of the time. When the retailer processes the fraudulent coupons many – if not all – coupons are returned unpaid. Retailers can control the cost of fraud by loading fraudulent coupon definitions provided by Coupon Information Corporation (CIC) to the POS, but this process is time-consuming and costly. The fraud database needs to be updated on a daily basis to stay current with the published fraudulent coupons. And many of the retailers have limits on the number of fraudulent coupon definitions that can be maintained on the POS.

Last year, the CIC dealt with more than 300 instances of coupon fraud costing millions of dollars. The estimated cost to the retailer of the undetected fraudulent coupons is $60 to $90 per store per month. The problem is large and appears to be growing, due to the ability to multiply fraudulent coupons on the internet; the availability of high-quality, low-cost printers; and the proliferation of counterfeit couponing, now estimated to be a $325-$500 million yearly problem for the CPG industry alone. With the introduction of the new GS1 Databar coupon standard, which became effective in 2012, coupons contain more information than the old UPC-A barcodes, in part to control mis/mal-redemption, but not fraud.

A real-time fraud prevention service would support the new GS1 Databar coupons and eliminate the need for retailers to manage fraudulent coupon definitions at the POS. This saves the retailer time and money. To assist in the fraud detection, this real-time service would enable manufacturers to create a positive file of valid coupons. This positive file would move the coupon world into the new millennium and out of the '80s. Any coupon presented at the POS that does not match one in the master file is automatically rejected. The manufacturers would also provide a coupon rule set to be followed when the real-time service validates manufacturer's coupons. As an example, one rule could be that the manufacturer does not distribute coupons over $10 in value.

New Controls
Here are some of the controls that can be implemented readily through real-time coupon validation:

- Attain a complete and updated family code file. This file would be updated by the CPG manufacturers and centrally controlled. This central family code database would not only benefit the manufacturers by ensuring proper validation at the retailers POS, but also give the retailers—for the first time—a complete and accurate file.

- Enable an independent third party to read and validate coupons in real time at the retailers' POS. This independent third party would ensure for both the retailers and the manufacturers that each coupon is redeemed under the criteria set by the manufacturer to ensure a 100% payment to the retailer. Real-time coupon validation would track:

    o At the family code level

    o GS1 Databar coupons

    o Expired coupons

    o That sufficient items are purchased (buy 2 get "x" off)

    o Identify fraud, both fraudulent coupons and cashier fraud.

To date, efforts to attain and enable the POS to validate at the family code level have been unsuccessful. The main issue is that the manufacturers have not put the needed effort into keeping the files up to date, since retailers are not validating at the family code level. This vicious circle has not abated over time.

Once a central family code file is available, things will be considerably easier. This central file will be able to alert manufacturers when the database is missing products. Manufacturers will be able to quickly research problems and update the family code database from one central point. This would enable all the retailers on the central real-time validation network to be updated at once. As the check environment improved once the ACH system became standard, family code validation will improve once a central database becomes standard. This will also save millions in family code maintenance cost for both retailers and manufacturers.

The GS1 Databar has an important place in improving POS validation. But if we do not have the ability or desire to read and use the information from the Databar during the validation process, all could be wasted. In this new electronic world, the independent third party would use the Databar and have the ability to report complete redemption details to both retailers and manufacturers.

Other Potential Capabilities

Another advantage of moving beyond the industry's present '80s technology for paper coupons is to provide complete real-time processing for all digital, mobile and direct-to-card promotions and offers, with the following additional functionality:

Coupon Arbitration: Digital to digital and digital to paper. Coupon arbitration would control deal stacking. Many manufacturers may start to require coupon arbitration before they will provide digital content for a retailer's direct-to-card program.

Targeted Email: Retailers could mail targeted emails weekly. Again, the real-time service would execute the targeted promotions without retailers' IT involvement. Real-time reporting would give retailers accurate usage that would be available to enhance the targeting of future emails.

Private Label: Retailers could promote weekly digital offers for their private label brands using the electronic promotion manager. This would enhance the total value of offers available to the retailer's shopper while increasing their private label product movement.

Managing Complex Promotions: The real-time solution would help retailers execute any of the following complex promotions by Units, Weight, or Dollars Spent and more without any of the limits from their existing POS:

- ***Buy Product A, Buy Product B, Get Instant Savings on Product C:***

    1. ***Bonus Promotions***: Link an endless number of promotions, creating a tiered promotion capability. The more you redeem, the more you save.

    2. ***Threshold Promotions***: Get up to # of Product "B" free when you first buy # of Product "A."

    3. ***Tracking Promotions***: Track purchase activity in real time and trigger a separate event like automatic activation of a digital promotion loaded to the customer's card. This is also useful for real-time tracking of new product introductions.

- ***Department, Category or Brand Buy/Units, Weight, or Dollars***

The coupon industry is ready for change. A complete real-time coupon validation is on the horizon.

Jon Robertson is Executive Vice President of Marketing for the Intelligent Clearing Network. For more information: www.icn-net.com

CHAPTER 19

Satisfying Customer Need for Accurate and Relevant Product Information for Today and Beyond

By Randy Burd

Shopping no longer requires a trip to a brick-and-mortar store, as many consumers are choosing to make their purchases with just a couple of clicks. Millennials, the major force in online purchasing, represent more than 95 million people in the U.S. alone. Their buying decisions are being based on product research in preparation for purchases and for health and well-being purposes.

With the demand for high-quality images and reliable data growing at a very rapid pace, and because their importance is spreading to all shopping experiences, the hunt is on for the most dynamic and economically feasible way for retailers, e-tailers, and Internet application developers (IADs) to obtain content, and for brand owners to protect the integrity of the brands they have worked so hard to build.

History
The need for product information is getting all the buzz now, but the need for visual product representations (images) has been around for years. In the 1990s, there was a huge influx of venture capital money

being poured into e-commerce grocery companies, all searching for the right model and competing for a share in the booming online shopping industry. No matter what the business model was, they all had two basic needs where content was concerned: Good quality images, and accurate, comprehensive product information. With so much attention being paid to site development, logistics, marketing, and relationships with vendors, in some cases the actual content became an afterthought, often leaving companies scrambling to meet rollout commitments.

Current State of Data Collection/Distribution
When people think of product information, the first things that leap to mind are ingredient statements and nutritional facts. These are, indeed, extremely important, but they are also a very small subset of a complete product profile.

Romance copy and "why buy" lines are used for bullets on e-commerce sites. Physical dimensions and weights are needed to calculate picking orders, shipping configurations and costs. Preparation and safe handling instructions, warnings and indications, and information about where the product and/or ingredients originate are all examples of product information that at one time was viewed as nice to have, but not a necessity. That has all changed.

So where do the necessary content components to represent products online come from? Too often, in the interest of saving time and money, products are hastily profiled and photographed in less than ideal conditions to "get something online now." Images are often very poor quality or are not originated by professionals and may appear non-dimensional or skewed. Also, data sets generally do not contain the full host of information found on the product label.

Where Does It All Come From?
IADs assume product images and data exist somewhere; they simply need to find out where to get them. This is true, but there is often great expense involved, unless the products in question are sponsored by the

vendor and included in a freely distributed program, or if vendors have already done the work themselves of hosting content for their customers to access (which not many do).

Retailers looking to populate their own online initiatives would turn to their ad departments for content, only to find out the sizes, resolutions, and formats of available images were not consistent with what is needed for a web environment. Plus, there was virtually no product information available at the advertising level. It became evident that content needed to drive web and mobile apps had to meet certain specifications, and was needed for all products being sold – not just feature items advertised on a somewhat regular basis.

Some tried to use planogram databases, but planogram images are shot straight on and have no dimension the way more visually appealing marketing shots do. And the planogram approach still leaves the issue of not having a comprehensive data set.

The Data Dilemma

There are many challenges when it comes to product information. Consistency across all products, cost, accuracy, and keeping content up-to-date plague the entire trade. Some of the practices to try and get around these challenges compound the problem. For example:

- ***Data Mining and Harvesting***: Sometimes companies resort to scanning the web in search of usable images and data. This just multiplies the problem of poor quality images and incomplete data being used.

- ***Short-Sighted Data Aggregation***: Comprehensive data aggregation requires profiling skills and the right tools to be done properly. There is much more to it than filling out a few columns in a spreadsheet. Specific image and data requirements published by a retailer or e-tailer often do not necessarily jive with what the next retailer or e-tailer will need. This puts the burden on vendors and data aggregators to create different processes to satisfy the needs of different customers, wasting precious time and resources.

- ***Locating All Pertinent Data Points Under One Roof:*** Most think the path of least resistance to get accurate product information would be for vendors to simply serve up the data for their own products themselves, since they have to have all of it for the product label. That's much easier said than done; different data elements are often the responsibility of different departments, and bringing it all together presents quite the logistical challenge. Even for those vendors who do pull that off, there is still the matter of getting suitable quality images created and into the hands of the people who need them at the same time as the associated product data.

- ***Different Departments, Different Needs:*** Another issue brand owners face is application segmentation within their own organizations. Too often the need for marketing content is handled by one department, space management content by another, and e-commerce by yet another. Each department operates with their own specific budgets, goals, and objectives, and that leads to tremendous inefficiencies. In reality, images are used in a variety of applications, and not all sizes, resolutions, or styles/angles of shots work for all of them. The philosophy of satisfying varying data and image requirements for ALL applications – while touching the product only once – is the best and most efficient way to ensure all segments of the industry using images and data have exactly what they need, when they need it.

Best Practices Moving Forward

Establishing and enforcing standards is the only way to ensure consistency and efficiencies across an industry where there are so many potential providers and users of content. GS1 efforts are helping to get everyone on the same page at the same time. Kwikee has been involved as a Solution Partner and has worked with establishing product image specifications and business-to-consumer data aggregation and distribution.

GS1's first and main focus was on business-to-business transactional data, but it has started moving rapidly toward defining data collection and delivery standards for business-to-consumer applications.

The revenue potential of online and mobile shopping, and the need for rich content for social media marketing is reason enough for this rapid move. But the need to get standards established and in place on a global scale has been punctuated by new regulations developed by the European Union (EU). The EU has published regulations for selling products online that will come into force in December of 2014. Basically, any product information available on a product's label must be presented to a consumer when viewing that product in an online or mobile buying environment.

These regulations are not slated to go into effect in the U.S. at that same time, but similar regulations could be coming in the future. They are also a concern for any company marketing and selling products globally. For more information on GS1 Source and the TSD initiative, please visit www.gs1.org.

The Most Reliable Source

The single most reliable and accurate source of product information is the product itself. Having access to a physical sample, then running that sample through a highly defined photographic, product profiling, and quality control process, is the most effective way to deliver a comprehensive set of both images and data.

Images are used in a variety of applications, and not all sizes, resolutions, or styles/angles of shots work for all of them. Satisfying the varying requirements for all applications while touching the product only once is yet another reason data aggregators need to be provided physical product samples.

Keeping product content up-to-date as packaging is revised and data changes is equally important. It can be frustrating, and very expensive, unless you work with an aggregator that fully understands the need to enable image and data updates and provides a seamless way to stream the updates in a painless and cost-effective manner.

All brand owners are not in the position to dedicate production resources to photography and data aggregation efforts. And retailers and e-tailers are not in the position to attempt to fund the population of images and data, let alone trying to manage keeping it all up-to-date. As with many other specialized services commonly outsourced, companies that specialize in data aggregation and photographic services are a wise investment. As mentioned earlier, photographic techniques and data collection tools and best practices continue to evolve, and keeping up with it all can be a daunting task.

Randy Burd is the product manager for Kwikee, a division of MultiAd, a provider of product imaging and data capture processes, content aggregation and distribution. For more information: www.Kwikeesystems.com and rburd@kwikeesystems.com.

INDEX

3D, 149

Accenture, 93-4, 132, 170
ACH, 182, 186
Acme, 42
Acquisition, 46, 159
Agent-Based Modeling (ABM), 112, 113, 114, 115, 117
Ahonen, Tomi, 172
AIR MILES, 27-9
Aisle Bump-Out, 78
Albertson's, 42
ALDI, 140, 142
Alice.com, 165
Allen, Wade, 179
Amazon, 16, 19, 22, 33, 34, 35, 93, 139, 168
AMG Strategic Advisors, 116
Apache, 132
Apple, 173
Arnold, 55
Asplund, Jim, 31
At-Shelf Behavior, 73, 80

Bread, 79, 81-2
Balakrishnan, Venky, 134
Barcode, 176, 177, 178, 185
Bassett, Kent, 80
Bed Bath & Beyond, 40
Behavioral Data, 73, 98
Belly, 45
Best Buy, 33, 139
Bhothinard, Tanya, 48
Big Bang, 94
Big Data, ii, iii, iv, 72, 73, 74, 76, 77, 79, 80, 81, 82, 83, 98, 101, 102, 103, 107, 119-21, 123-5, 128, 129, 130, 131, 132, 133, 134, 157
Bleach It Away Campaign, 53-4
Blog, 6, 7, 54, 64, 120, 163, 165, 166, 167, 168
Booz & Company, 86
Borders, 139
Brand Communities, iii, 50, 51, 53, 54, 56

Brand Comparison Index, 77
Brand Experience, 35, 43, 148, 154
Brandsavers, 45
Brick-and-Mortar, 45, 72, 82, 128, 130, 138, 140, 189
Bricks Meets Clicks Research, 89
Brownberry, 55
Burd, Randy, 194
Burd, Steve, 44
Burke, Ray, 144-5
Burns, Larry, 161
Business Intelligence, 120

CalorieCount.com, 165
Cartwheel, 41
Catalina, 172, 173
Category Management, 79, 81, 82, 97, 132, 133, 136, 144, 146
Check Validation, 181, 183
Chicklet, 173
Childs, Nancy, 96
Christensen, Clayton, 91-2
Circuit City, 139
Circular, 40, 43, 88, 127, 164, 173
Clearing House, 177
Clip Unit, 173
Clorox, 53-4, 56
Club Stores, 9, 138
Coffee, 6, 41, 140-1, 154
Cole, Steve, 169
COLLOQUY, 39, 44
Communities of Consent, iv, 99, 100
ConAgra, 159
Concierge, 165
Consumer Journey, 144
Consumer Network Panel, 5
Consumer Packaged Goods (CPG), ii, iii, iv, v, 3, 4, 6, 7, 8, 9, 40, 42, 49, 51, 56, 71-2, 79, 82, 83, 97, 106, 107, 112, 123, 144, 145, 146, 147, 150, 156, 167, 171, 173, 185
Convenience Stores, 80, 81
Conversion Rate, 75, 77, 80, 81, 157
Cost-Per-Acquisition, 159
Coupon Arbitration, 187

Coupon Information Corporation (CIC), 184
Coupons, i, v, 4, 6, 7, 8, 11, 12, 15, 17, 18, 19, 20-3, 40, 41, 44, 45, 63, 86, 88, 95, 127, 132, 165, 168, 171-4, 175-8, 182-8
Coupons Inc., 173
Crowd Sourcing, 106
Customer Relationship Management (CRM), 134, 172

Dassault Systemes, 149, 150
Data Aggregation, v, 191, 193, 194
Data Mining, 191
Data Warehouse/Warehousing, 120, 121
Demand Signal Repository (DSR), 120
Demographics, 72
Department of Defense, 72
Department of Homeland Security, 72
Devine, John, 144
Diapers, 7, 8, 54, 93
Diapers.com, 48
Dick's Sporting Goods, 141
Digital Coupon, i, v, 23, 175, 183
Digital Media, 5, 6, 7, 11, 22, 52, 86
Direct Mail, 28, 29, 127, 178
Direct-to-Card, 187
Display, i, 63, 72, 74, 75, 76, 78, 81, 127, 149
Disruptive Innovation, 91, 93, 95
Dorenkott, Janet, 125
Dorf, David, 130
Dr Pepper, ii
Duhigg, Charles, 65

Ebates, 45
eBay, 8, 168
Edgell Knowledge Network, 130
EDI, 122
Effort-Based Savings, ii, 16
Email, 6, 39, 47, 62, 64, 86, 87, 89, 124, 156, 173, 187
End Cap, 78, 81-2
Engagement, 78, 79, 98, 99, 104-5, 107, 143, 144, 149, 156

Enjoy the Ride Rewards, 40-1, 44, 45
Enterprise Loyalty, iii, 33, 36
Entitlement-Based Loyalty, ii, 16
e-Sampling, 154, 155, 158, 159, 160
Etsy, 8
European Union (EU), 193
Executional Excellence, 143
Expediting, 143, 149

Facebook, ii, 6, 7, 11, 12, 41, 52, 54, 55, 89, 130, 132, 134, 154, 156, 158
Family Code, 183, 185, 186-7
Family Rewards, ii
FatWallet, 45
Five Stars, 45
Fleming, John, 31
Food Lion, 51, 52, 56
Food Marketing Institute (FMI), 86, 96
FoodEssentials.com, 165
Foodland, 11
Frankel, Bethenny, 54
Fraud/Fraudulent, 173, 177, 181, 182, 183-4, 185, 186
Free Standing Insert (FSI), 173, 178
Frequent Shopper Card, 42, 44, 128, 134, 157
Fresh & Easy, 11
Fresh Direct, 139
FunMobility, 172, 174

Gallup, 31, 32
Geo-Targeting, 11
Gilmore, James, 140
Gilt Group, 34
Gladson, 168, 169
Gluten-Free, 165, 166
Gmail, 11
Google, 67, 68, 70, 130, 161, 168
GreenBook Research, 100
Grocery Apps, 87, 91, 92, 93, 94, 95
Grocery Shopping, iii, 21, 85, 86, 87, 88, 89, 90-5, 139, 164, 170
Grocery Store/Supermarket, i, iv, 9, 11, 40, 41, 42, 73, 80, 81, 89, 91, 138, 141, 142, 146, 176

GS1, 185, 186, 187, 192, 193
Gupta, Sanjiv, 116

Hadoop, 119, 132
Happy Feet, 41
Harinarayan, Venky, 127
Hartman Group, 88-9
Heat Map, 80
Hispanic Shoppers, 22, 80
Home Depot, 174
Home Made Simple, 156
Household Panel Data, 71, 74
Huggies, 40-1, 44, 45
Hutton, Ellie, 108

IBM, 102
Impression Delivery, 158
Impulse Purchase, 81
Inmar Analytics, 16, 17, 19, 20, 22, 23, 172, 173
Insight Communities, iv, 99, 100, 101, 103, 107
Instagram, 55, 87
In-Store Behavior, iii, 72-3, 74, 79, 80, 81, 83
Intelligent Clearing Network (ICN), 188
Internet, 4, 5, 6, 7, 17, 64, 67, 68, 72, 86, 130, 163, 172, 175, 185, 189
Internet Application Developers (IAD), 189, 190
IRI, 5, 10, 13, 122, 161, 170
ISIS, 172

JC Penney, 139
JDE, 120
Jewel, 41, 42
Johnson and Johnson, 146
Just For U, i, 42, 44

Kantar Retail Power Ranking, 82
Kellogg, ii, 146
Khan, Mickey Alam, 166
Kimberly-Clark, 146, 159
Kirkland, 41
Kraft, 159

Kroger, 11, 44, 46
Kwikee, 192, 194

Lavine, Adam, 174
Lean Cuisine Delicious Rewards, 43
Like-Gating, 154
LinkedIn, 7
Load-to-Card, 175, 178
Logistics, 168, 190
Long-Haul Shoppers, 73
Loyalty Data, 71, 124
Loyalty Programs, i, ii, 21, 27, 39-47, 138
LoyaltyOne, 27, 32, 36
Luvs, 41

Malredemption/Misredemption, 178, 184, 185
Mansumer, 21, 22
Market Force Information/Survey, 139, 141
Market Research, 99, 100, 104, 160
Marketing Mix Modeling (MMM), 111-6
m-Assisted Retailing/Shopping, iii, 88, 91, 94
McKinsey & Company, 89-90, 144
Meat, 33, 39
Meijer, 40
Menards, 43, 47
Mercatus Technology, 165
Metro, i
Millennials, 22, 93, 189
Mills, C. Wright, 50
Mobile App, 68, 85, 91, 128, 135, 163, 164, 167, 174, 191
Mobile Coupon Ad Standards Unit (MoCAUS), 171
Mobile Marketing Association (MMA), v, 166, 171, 174
Moment of Truth, 66, 67, 71, 72, 73, 76, 77, 82, 156, 161, 170
Mommy Blogs, 165, 168
MonaBar, 45
mPerks, 40-1

Mueller, Trish, 174
MultiAd, 194
Multi-Channel Shopper, v, 49, 56, 163, 166, 169
My Coke Rewards, 39, 41-2, 43, 46
My Essentials, 52, 53
My Very Best, 156
MySpace, 11

National Do Not Call Registry, 62
National Grocers Association (NGA), 89, 90
National Science Foundation, 72
Navigation Complexity, 77
Nestle, 156
New Egg, 45
Newhook, Robin, 56-7
Newspaper, i, 15, 44, 64, 67, 127, 170
North Carolina, 52

Office Depot, 45, 47
Ogilvy Group, 128
Online Grocery Shopping, 89, 91, 139
Online Sampling, 153, 154, 156, 157, 159, 160
Operation Grocery Drop, 51-2
Oracle, 121
Oroweat, 55
Owned Media, 156

Paid Media, 156
Pampers, 41, 43, 44, 45
Partners in Loyalty Marketing, 40, 48
Passbook, 173
Path to Purchase, 66-7, 72, 73, 74, 75, 80, 88, 153, 156
Pearson, Bryan, 36
Peck Fellowship, 86, 96
Peck Research, 90, 92, 95
PepsiCo, 42, 79, 80-1, 83
Perka, 45
Perkville, 45
PetSmart, 45
Pew Research Center/American Life Project, 93, 170, 172

Piggly Wiggly, 138
Pine, Joseph, 140
Planogram, 73, 74, 107, 146, 147, 148-9, 191
PointsPlus, 55
POS, 10, 122-4, 171, 173, 175, 176, 177, 182-7
Pottery Barn, 40
Predictive Modeling, 79, 102
Price Optimization, 138, 144, 145
PriceWaterhouseCoopers, 89
Print-at-Home, 175, 178
Private Label, 187
Problem Recovery, 173
Procter & Gamble (P&G), 45, 46, 132, 145-6, 156, 159
Publix, 139, 141
Purchase Data, 94, 157

QR Code, i, 91, 173
Quick Service Restaurant (QSR), 98
Quick Trip, 80

Rebates, 9, 43
Recession, 47, 139, 142
Red Laser Scanning, 171, 173
Regression-Based Modeling (RBM), 111, 113, 114
REI, 141
Relational Solutions, 125
Retail Council of Canada, 143
Retention, 46, 104
Rewards Program, 41, 159
Reynolds, Kyle, 81
Right at Home, 156
Ring, Rafe, 128
Robertson, Jon, 188
ROI, 9, 12, 49, 53, 54, 55, 72, 82, 99, 106, 107, 116, 155, 156
Ross, John, 23

Safeway, i, 42, 44, 139, 168
Sainsbury, 146
Sampling, iv, 56, 153-60
Sandwich Thins, 54, 55, 56

SAP, 120
Sara Lee, 79, 81-2, 83
SC Johnson, 156
Scan & Go, 134
Scanning, 171, 173, 176, 177, 181, 183, 184, 191
Sears, 41, 139
Seattle, 139
Seattle's Best Coffee, 154
Segmentation, ii, 5, 11, 192
Seiberling, Eric, 150
Senter, Kimberly, 146
Sharma, Dr. Rajeev, 83
Shaw's, 42
Shea, Dr. Michael, 116
Shell Oil, 27-30
Shop Your Way Rewards, 41
Shopper, i, iii, iv, 3-12, 15-23, 61-70, 71-83, 86-95, 97, 99, 104, 107, 128, 129, 134, 135, 136, 137-150, 157, 159-60, 163-6, 169, 170, 183, 187
Shopper Behavior, iii, 17, 22, 63, 71-2, 74, 80, 81, 131
Shopper Engagement, iii, 61, 65, 70
Shopper Insights, 80, 81, 82, 132
Shopper Leakage, 75-6
Shopper Marketing, 3, 9, 10, 16, 66, 71-2, 79, 82, 133, 135
Shopper Technology, ii, v
Shopper Technology Institute, v, 40, 81
Shopper-Centric, 77, 146
Shopper-to-Buyer Conversion, 75, 81
Shopping Time, 77, 78
Showrooming, 137-8, 148
Signage, 78, 82, 148
Smartphone, i, iii, iv, 6, 7, 8, 16, 22, 23, 66, 68, 85, 86-7, 89, 90, 91, 93, 94, 95, 131, 153, 164, 170
SMS, 173
Social Media, i, ii, iii, 4, 6, 7, 12, 49-56, 64, 65, 85, 87, 88, 98, 99, 103-4, 120, 122, 124, 131, 134, 135, 155, 156, 158, 163, 164, 167, 193
Soft Sheen, 154
SoMoLoMe, 128, 129, 131, 134, 136

Space Planning, 79, 133, 146
SPAM, 62, 69
Spotzot, 172
Sprecher, Ben, 70
Sprint-Nextel, 172
Staples, 45
Starbucks, 41, 141
Start Sampling, 154, 155, 159, 161
Stimulus, 66, 67, 156
Stone, Dorian, 144
Structured Data, 119-21, 124
Supermarkets, 15, 80, 142
Sur La Table, 141
Symphony IRI, 161

Tablet, iv, 66, 153, 172
Target, 41, 123, 168
Teavana, 41
Technophobe, 6, 7, 8, 12
Tenser, James, 136
Teradata, 119, 121
Tesco, 33, 34, 35, 123
Text, 87, 89, 119, 129, 174
Text/Short-Code Programs, 22
Thanks Again, 45
Time Productivity, 78
Tomei, Bob, 13
Tosolini, Alex, 132
Toys "R" Us, 45
Trade Promotion, 72, 82, 138, 144
Trader Joe's, 139, 141, 142
Traffic, 49, 75, 78, 81, 82, 141
Transaction Data, 71, 98, 102, 103, 107, 157, 193
Transactions, 131, 142, 144, 174, 176, 177, 182, 184
Tribune, 172
Tweet, 64, 87
Twitter, ii, 7, 52, 54, 120, 131, 156, 158

Unilever, 146
Univision, 172
Unstructured Data, 119, 121, 124
UPC-A Barcode, 185
URL, 156, 173

Valassis, 173
Valpak, 172, 178
Validation, v, 100, 101, 115, 174, 181, 183-8
Value, ii, 16, 19, 20, 30, 31, 32, 52, 55, 78, 85, 91, 93, 94, 95, 99, 103, 104, 120, 121, 132, 140, 154, 158, 187
Verde, 143
Video Sensors, 73
VideoMining, 72, 73, 74, 80, 83
Virtual Technology, ii, iv, 128, 144-7, 150
Vision Critical, 108
VLDB, 121
VSN Strategies, 136

Wal-Mart, 121, 123, 134-5, 139, 140, 141, 146
Walmart, 44, 127, 131, 134-5, 138, 157
Webvan, 139
Wegmans, 139, 142
Weight Watchers, 54-5
West Virginia, 11
Wharton, 143
Whole Foods, 11, 139, 141

Yahoo, 21, 172
YouTube, 11, 154

Zappos, 34, 47, 48

CPSIA information can be obtained at www.ICGtesting.com
Printed in the USA
LVOW10s1443061213

364195LV00002B/50/P